THE CONSTRUCTION OF
HADRIAN'S WALL

THE CONSTRUCTION OF
HADRIAN'S WALL

PETER HILL

TEMPUS

First published 2006

Tempus Publishing Limited
The Mill, Brimscombe Port,
Stroud, Gloucestershire, GL5 2QG
www.tempus-publishing.com

British Library Cataloguing in Publication Data.
A catalogue record for this book is available from the British Library.

ISBN 0 7524 4011 X

Typesetting and origination by Tempus Publishing Limited
Printed in Great Britain

CONTENTS

GLOSSARY

Arris	The distinct line or edge formed by the meeting of two worked surfaces
Ashlar	Stone which is carefully worked to give a very clean appearance with fine joints, and with all corners forming a right angle
Bed (1)	The height of stone in a quarry between breaks in sedimentary deposition or change in the character of the sediment
Bed (2)	The upper or lower surface of a stone, or the bedding material on which the stone rests
Bedding of stone	1. Natural bedded. Stone laid in the same orientation in which is was originally laid down 2. Face bedded. Stone laid so that the natural bedding planes are set vertically, parallel to the surface of the wall 3. Edge bedded. Where the stone is laid with the bedding planes set at right angles to the surface of the wall
Carver	One who works stone to freehand designs, abstract, foliage, or figure
Centre	A wooden framework on which the voussoirs of an arch are built
Circular-circular-sunk	A moulding or feature which is convex in both directions; the interior of a bowl is an example
Column	A circular shaft supporting a lintel or arch
Crown	The highest point of an arch
Dimension stone	Stone which is to be worked to a specific size. In the context of the Wall this is limited to gate piers,

	voussoirs, cornices, and similar items; it does not relate to the facing stones or to the string course
Draft	Any worked strip on the surface of a stone; it may be straight or curved to match the profile of a templet. A marginal draft runs along the edge of the surface
Dressed stone	Worked to a specified shape, but 'roughly dressed' is quite different
Drum	One stone in a column made up of several stones
Entasis	The slight convexity of a column shaft
Extrados	The outer (upper) curved outline of an arch
Fixing	Placing stones in position on a building
Footings	Projecting courses at foot of wall etc.
Foundation	Solid ground or base, natural or artificial, on which building rests; lowest part of building, usually below ground level
Glacis	Outer side of ditch where excavated material is spread to form a slope
Impost	Projecting stone on which an arch rests
Intrados	The inner (lower) curved outline of an arch. See also *Soffit*
Joint	1. The vertical side of a stone, against which another is placed
	2. The mortar in the space between two adjacent stones
	3. A natural crack or fault in a quarry, running vertically down through the beds. See also *Shake*
Kivel	A form of scappling hammer, with hammer and pick ends
Laggings	Short battens, connecting the two sides of a centre, on which the voussoirs rest
Moulded	Stone with a moulding worked on it
Moulding	The profile formed by working a stone to an ornamental section
Overburden	The non-stone material, soil, flaggy stone etc., overlying the sought-after beds of stone
Pier	The support for an arch or lintel, usually square or rectangular in section
Pinch bar	Small crowbar
Pozzolanic	Material such as volcanic sand or fired clay added to lime to produce hydraulic mortar

Quoin	Stone worked to form the corner of a building
Raking joint	The temporary end of a length of wall, where the ends of each course are successively set back
Return	A change of direction on the face of a stone, usually at right angles. An external return is formed of two outer faces of a stone. An internal return has the angle cut into the stone
Reveal	The surface of the side of an opening
Rf	Roman foot (*pes Monetalis*)
Roughed-out	A stone in which the major waste has been removed prior to completion to a finished form
Roughly dressed	Usually used to describe stone given an approximate shape with simple tools such as punch or walling hammer
Scapple/scabble	To roughly square up a quarried block, using a scappling hammer
Sculptor	An artistic carver
Shake	An internal crack or fissure in timber
Skelp	Waste pieces of any size resulting from working stone
Soffit	The underside of an arch or overhanging eaves
Span	The horizontal distance between the lowest parts of an arch; the distance between the piers
Springer	The lowest voussoir in an arch
Stilted	An arch in which the curve begins one or more courses above the impost
String course	A thin course of stone, usually moulded, which projects beyond the wall line and is generally designed to shed water
Templet	Pattern made in rigid material showing the shape to which a stone is to be worked
Voussoir	A wedge-shaped stone forming part of an arch
Worked stone	Also dressed, but not same as 'roughly dressed'
Working/dressing	Shaping stone to a specified form. Strictly speaking, squared rubble is not worked stone as the final size is approximate

PREFACE

This book is based on the author's 2002 doctoral thesis in the University of Durham, published in 2004 as *The Construction of Hadrian's Wall* (*BAR* British Series 375). As this is not easily accessible for the general reader, the present volume has been written in order to present the research to the wider public. So as to fit it into a volume of half the length, many of the details have had to be simplified, but it is hoped that there will be sufficient content to satisfy the interested visitor.

Use has, of course, been made of the work of others, but to avoid cluttering the text the majority of references will be found in the chapter bibliographies at the end. The full bibliography, as well as detailed argument, will be found in the *BAR* volume.

This book is in no way a guide to the Wall, and its history is covered only as essential background to the building. The best general history of the Wall and the northern frontier is *Hadrian's Wall* by David J. Breeze and Brian Dobson (Fourth edition, 2000). For a detailed guide to the remains see *Handbook to the Roman Wall* by J.C. Bruce (Fourteenth edition revised by David J. Breeze 2006). Both these works are essential for any serious study of the Wall.

There will be constant reference to milecastles and turrets by number. The system was devised by R.G. Collingwood in 1931, with numbers running from east to west, and is explained at the beginning of chapter 2.

Inscriptions from the Wall are mostly published in *The Roman Inscriptions of Britain* and referred to by number, e.g. *RIB* 1647.

One of the problems with the study of Hadrian's Wall is that in practice very little is known about it. The Stone Wall originally had 49 milecastles (MC0-MC48) and 96 turrets, and on the Turf Wall there were 32 milecastles and 62 turrets. The interiors of 8 milecastles out of 80 have been extensively investigated. In at least one milecastle, MC42, no evidence of Roman buildings was found.

Around two dozen turrets out of 159 have been fully excavated. Some very early excavations were limited, uncovering the remains at a time when there was scant understanding of stratigraphy. The 17 forts which were eventually part of the Wall complex have received comparatively greater attention, but to date only one of these, Wallsend, has been fully excavated.

Today, there are few structures where any masonry is visible: 7 milecastles (10, 33, 35, 37, 39, 42, 48), 14 stone wall turrets and 3 turf wall turrets (7b, 26b, 29a, 33b, 34a, 35a, 36b, 39b, 41a, 44b, 45a, 48a, 48b, 49b, 51a, 51b, 52a) with 2 additional towers (Peel Gap and Pike Hill), and 7 forts (Wallsend, Chesters, Housesteads, Vindolanda, Greatchesters, Carvoran, Birdoswald); in some cases the visible remains are fragmentary. In addition there are several miles of curtain wall, ranging from the tiny fragment in a garage forecourt at the junction of Westgate Road and Denton Road in Newcastle upon Tyne, to the long stretches over Cuddy's Crag and Walltown Crags.

Almost all the remains are unsatisfactory, to a greater or lesser extent, in the evidence they provide. Some lengths of curtain wall were rebuilt, in part at least, by John Clayton in the nineteenth century, as were parts of the fort at Housesteads and the turret at Brunton, T26b. Since his day, considerable lengths of the curtain have been exposed and consolidated by the Ministry of Works and its successors, the Department of the Environment and English Heritage. The greater part of this was carried out with only minimal archaeological supervision until the late 1970s, and much of the detail is known only from the careful records kept by the late Charles Anderson in his role as site foreman.

A further problem is caused by the fact that from Newcastle to around MC33 the remains of the Wall were demolished in the eighteenth century to form the base for a new road, at the request of the army who had suffered from the lack of good communication between Newcastle and Carlisle during the 1745 rebellion. It is still known as the Military Road.

Measurements are normally given in metric units and follow the system used in the building trade: measurements below 10m are given in millimetres, and centimetres are not used at all. Approximate conversion to Imperial measure is given as well as to Roman measure. The Roman foot (*pes Monetalis*) used in the building was equal to 296mm or approximately 11⅝ inches. The Roman mile was 1480m or 1618yds long. A tonne is only 17kg (37lb) less than the ton, and conversions are not given.

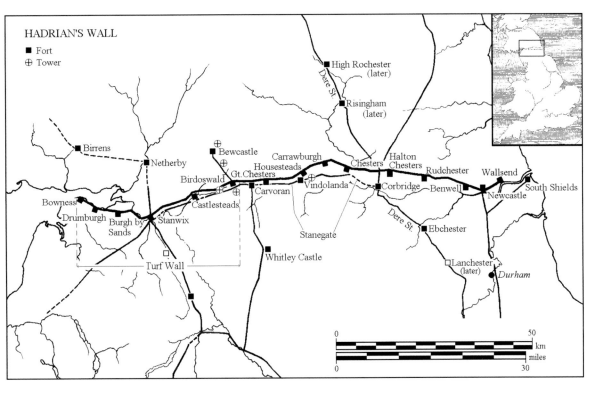

1 Map of Hadrian's Wall

THE ROMAN ARMY

The Roman army was made up of two basic kinds of troops. The legions were composed of Roman citizens, who in theory could come from anywhere in the empire, and consisted of around 4800 heavy infantry. They were divided into centuries of 80 men, grouped into 10 cohorts of 6 centuries, although there are some problems with this organisation which are discussed in chapter 9.

The auxiliaries were not normally Roman citizens but were recruited originally from allies and newly conquered provinces, and usually had a name reflecting their ethnic origin. The infantry units were cohorts of either 6 or 10 centuries, again of 80 men each, with a strength of 480 or 800 men. Cavalry units were divided into 16 troops (*turmae*) of around 30 men; there were a small number of larger units, no more than one to a province, with 24 troops. Some units were mixed cavalry and infantry.

The Wall was built by the legions, and manned by auxiliaries.

ACKNOWLEDGEMENTS

Many people have contributed directly and indirectly to both the research and the writing of the book, and the author is deeply indebted to them. Particular thanks are due to Dr David Breeze, who kindly commented on parts of the text, Dr Brian Dobson for many years of encouragement, and Professor Jenny Price who argued for this form of publication.

1

INTRODUCTION

OUTLINE HISTORY

After the abortive raids on Britain in 55 and 54 BC the Romans finally began the conquest of Britain in AD 43 under the direction of the Emperor Claudius. Over the next three decades the army pushed northwards at a speed usually dependent more on the will of the various emperors than on local conditions. The one exception was the rebellion of Boudica in the early AD 60s which led to a policy of slow consolidation in the area roughly to the south of a line from the Humber to the Dee. There may well have been some penetration to the north, but it was not until Petillius Cerialis became governor in AD 71 that the conquest resumed in a serious way.

He moved the Ninth legion from Lincoln to York as part of the campaign to overcome the Brigantes, the large tribe or confederation which occupied most of Derbyshire, Yorkshire, and Lancashire. It seems to have been Cerialis who established the route over the Pennines from Scotch Corner to Carlisle, and established a fort at the latter place in AD 73.

In the later AD 70s Gnaeus Julius Agricola was appointed governor with a mandate from the Emperor Vespasian to expand the province. After a hiatus caused by the death of Vespasian, progress was rapid and by AD 83 the army had marched deep into what is now Scotland and brought the tribes to battle at Mons Graupius, the location of which is uncertain but was possibly somewhere between Aberdeen and Inverness. After this, Agricola was recalled, having served twice the usual term as governor.

It was almost certainly his successor who began the building of a new legionary fortress at Inchtuthil on the River Tay. Work on this 50-acre base was perhaps in its second year when the trouble on the Rhine and the Danube caused the recall of the Second Adiutrix legion, then based in Chester, and the part-built fortress was demolished. It is likely that some auxiliary units were withdrawn with the legion, and Roman forces gradually withdrew into, and then south of, the lowlands of Scotland.

Trajan's Dacian wars in the early years of the second century called for more troops, and by around AD 105 all forts seem to have been behind a line between the estuaries of the Tyne and Solway.

Finds of pottery from the fortress at York show a marked reduction from around 110 and it may have been then that the Ninth legion was withdrawn from the province. With only two legions in garrison, it would hardly have been practicable to do anything other than limit the area of the province which was under direct Roman military control.

ROMAN FRONTIERS

Hadrian's Wall was merely one small part of the several thousand miles of boundary between the Roman empire and those tribes not under the direct control of Rome.

Rome always had need of frontiers, in the sense of a zone of interface with its neighbours, but at first these do not seem to have been permanent in a physical form. There was no sense in which the empire was considered by the Romans to have a limit; they saw the world as consisting of those parts they already occupied and those parts which they had not yet occupied. In the ancient world, linear barriers, whether rivers or artificial lines, tended to mark no more than the division between the directly administered and the indirectly controlled areas. Rome exercised a powerful influence on the affairs of peoples living beyond its borders.

One reason for the growth of more formal frontiers, from the later Augustan period onwards, was the need for emperors to prevent their generals from seeking military and political prestige except in circumstances where there was strict imperial control.

It was not always necessary or sensible to annexe areas of poor economic advantage when control could be exercised by other means. Rome did not directly administer every aspect of life in a conquered province, but instead grafted Roman administration onto existing 'local government' structures. Where these did not exist, permanent occupation was less attractive.

THE GROWTH OF ARTIFICIAL FRONTIERS

The Emperor Domitian established frontier works in Germany, consisting of a track and timber towers linking a line of forts. Under Trajan, fortlets were added to the line but it was probably Hadrian who took the step of adding a timber palisade.

There are four areas where artificial land barriers were introduced by Hadrian: Britain, Upper Germany and Raetia (between the Rhine and Danube), Dacia (Romania), and north Africa. However, none of these frontiers was a wholly closed system. Hadrian's Wall had gateways at every mile, while the palisade in Upper Germany had openings with fortlets alongside them, and the earth-built *limes Porolissensis* in Romania, and the dry-stone *Fossatum Africae* were discontinuous. In every case these 'frontiers' were simply one part of an extended zone of Roman control rather than a rigid boundary.

In northern Britain a series of towers and fortlets along the road from Falkirk to Perth has been interpreted as a frontier line, known as the Gask Ridge. It consists of a series of closely set towers (18 are known at the time of writing) with three known fortlets, running northwards to Ardoch and from there eastwards towards Perth. On the basis of very limited dating evidence it has been assigned to the Flavian period. It may have been built as part of Agricola's campaign,[1] although it has been suggested that it could have been started as early as the 70s under the governor Cerialis, about whose operations there is little historical evidence. This is at present speculation, but the system does seem to represent a very early frontier in Britain, and may be earlier than the towers on the German frontier.

THE DEVELOPMENT OF THE TYNE–SOLWAY FRONTIER

The Wall was the culmination of some four decades of development along the Tyne–Solway isthmus. First, it will be useful to look at the nature of the countryside.

The Wall divides into three very different geological sectors, east, central, and west. In the east, stretching from the coast to the North Tyne at Chesters, the underlying sandstone and gritstone is covered by glacial drift to a depth of up to 80m. This gives a flat or rolling land surface over which building will have presented no great problems. There are sufficient outcrops on the ridges to provide supplies of sandstone for building, although limestone is readily available only from Harlow Hill (near MC16) westwards.

The central sector, which geologically may be said to begin at the North Tyne, is dominated by the quartz-dolerite intrusion of the Whin Sill. Both to north and south of the line of the Wall are ample supplies of limestone and sandstone. The Sill is broken in several places by glacial spillways, most notably at Peel Gap which drained the glacial lake of Crag Lough.

The western sector begins around Birdoswald. Close to MC54 the geology changes to Permo-Triassic, heavily overlain by deep glacial deposits. The countryside is softer and kinder than that further east and will have made for easier building. However, building stone and limestone for mortar are less readily available close to the Wall, although the Gelt quarries lie 2.5 miles (4km) south of the Wall on a tributary of the River Irthing. These were certainly worked by the Roman (the only dating evidence is of the early third century), as was the Sherwood sandstone near Weatherall on the River Eden. West of Carlisle there are no bedrock exposures along the boulder clay and alluvial soil of the Solway Firth and the nearest stone to be found is well to the south.

TOPOGRAPHICAL DESCRIPTION

From Wallsend the line of the Wall runs westwards across what is now generally level ground, although there were formerly a number of small valleys, running at right angles to the line, which have been filled in. Stott's Pow, on the bank of which stood MC1, is but one example. The ground gradually rises to the summit of Byker Hill, around 60m (200ft), from where it falls towards the large, steep-sided valley of the Ouseburn. Close to Newcastle was the valley of Pandon Burn.

To the west of Newcastle the ground rises more or less evenly to the site of the fort at Benwell, 127m (415ft) above sea level, over a distance of some 2 miles. Thereafter, the ground undulates, gradually rising to just under 245m (800ft) at the start of the crags of the Whin Sill (T33b, Coesike). In this stretch there are only two long, severe, gradients on either side of the valley of the North Tyne at Chesters. Over the crags the Wall holds to the edge of the Whin Sill, rising to 375m (1230ft) at MC40, Winshields. In this sector access to the Wall for constructional purposes is very limited from the northern side, where there are nearly sheer cliffs; to the south the line is approached on the dip slope of the escarpment, giving access which varies between awkward and difficult. The line is broken in places by steep-sided nicks such as Peel Gap (west of T39a) and the slope on which T44b, Mucklebank, stands.

Immediately west of Carvoran the land dips down relatively gently into the valley of the River Irthing which it crosses by means of Willowford Bridge, after which it rises very sharply by over 33m (100ft) to Harrow Scar and Birdoswald, which stand 150m (500ft) above sea level. Over the next 10 miles the height falls to less than 25m (75ft), and thereafter continues to fall to the marshes west of Carlisle where the line of the Wall follows the edge of the estuary of the Solway to Bowness.

FLORA

There is growing evidence from pollen analysis of the nature of the countryside at the time the Wall was built. In the Bronze and early Iron Ages there was a series of clearances, most of which were followed by forest regeneration. At the end of the Iron Age there were considerable clearances, resulting in an open landscape similar to today. It appears that some areas of the Wall zone were already extensively cleared long before Hadrian's Wall was built, probably in the late Iron Age, but there was further clearance connected with Roman activity.

There are a number of sites where evidence of cultivation is provided by ard marks in the soil below and adjacent to the Wall; examples are Wallsend, Throckley, Wallhouses, and Carrawburgh. It is probable that a considerable part of the course of the Wall ran through land which was in current use for arable farming.

In summary, it may be said that the line chosen for the Wall ran through countryside which was largely cleared, for arable use in the east and pastoral in the west, interspersed with light tree-cover and denser thickets in the valleys. The fact that the western 30 miles of the Wall could be built in turf indicates that the area was already largely given over to grassland rather than woodland. The temperature was probably about the same as today, with a not dissimilar climate.

THE STANEGATE

At Carlisle a fort was founded using timbers cut in the winter of 72-3 under Petillius Cerialis, and Corbridge Red House, nearly a mile from the present site of Roman Corbridge, may have a similar origin. The Roman road running between these two sites is now known as the Stanegate. On this road there was also a fort at Vindolanda, dating to around AD 85, and also at Nether Denton which may have had been similar in date. A third fort, Carvoran, could also date to this time; it lies at the junction of the Maiden Way with the Stanegate, and its history might not directly relate to either the Stanegate or Hadrian's Wall. The forts at Corbridge, Vindolanda, Nether Denton and Carlisle are set a short day's march apart from each other.

Two fortlets were added to the line, Haltwhistle Burn and Throp; both are believed to date to the reign of Trajan, along with a fort at Old Church Brampton. The spacing of forts and fortlets between Brampton and Vindolanda was thus reduced to 2-3.5 miles. Other sites along the Stanegate have been suggested, but evidence is lacking.

Three towers are also known on, or within half a mile of, the line of the Stanegate, and have been seen as part of the 'Stanegate system'. These are at Birdoswald, Mains Rigg (Over Denton), and Barcombe. The date and purpose of these towers are not easy to determine.

Two towers now on the Wall are anomalous. Pike Hill, on the Wall but not in the sequence of Wall turrets, seems to have been built before the Wall which now abuts it. It is set at an angle so that its south-east face looks squarely towards Nether Denton, the north-east to Robin Hood's Butt on Gillalees. It is noteworthy that Pike Hill remained in commission when the Wall was built, although a turret at the standard spacing was built only 200m to the west. T45a, Walltown Crags East, is also different in construction from the Wall turrets, although it fits into the sequence of Wall structures. Like Pike Hill it has a ground floor doorway and no surrounding ditch, although the latter is a feature of isolated towers.

The known additional fortlets and towers are restricted to just over a third of the distance between Corbridge and Carlisle, 13.5 miles out of 38. They occur in very roughly the same area as the larger milecastles on Hadrian's Wall on either side of the River Irthing, from MC47 to MC54, of which some details are given chapter 2. Furthermore, in the second phase of Wall building, forts immediately east of this area are more closely spaced than the usual 6-7 miles.

There may have been a particular problem around and to the east of the Irthing valley, although Symonds has recently suggested that at least some of the large milecastles were the result of an early design which was rapidly changed.

THE WALL DECISION

Hadrian's biographer says that at the start of his reign, AD 117, 'the Britons could hardly be kept under Roman control.' The fighting seems to have been over by AD 119, and about three years later Hadrian visited the province where he 'put right many things, and was the first to build a wall 80 miles long which would separate the Romans from the barbarians' (*SHA*, Hadrian, 2). It is generally considered that the emperor's visit took place in AD 122, although there is no positive evidence for this date. The only fixed date for this period in Britain is the diploma (certificate of citizenship issued to an auxiliary soldier) of 17 July 122, recording A. Platorius Nepos as a very recently appointed governor

(*CIL* xvi, 65). This date has tended to attract other known events which are themselves undated: the transfer of legion VI to Britain and the visit of the emperor are seen as occurring in mid-122 in the absence of other evidence. Certainly emperor, governor and legion all travelled to Britain from Lower Germany.

It has been suggested that the Wall was begun one or two years before the emperor's visit, and that the decision to dig the Vallum and to move forts onto the line of the Wall was taken by Hadrian in person. However, the political implications of the primary decision, the rigidity of the design, and the enormous investment in labour, all point to the personal involvement of the emperor.

Given that there was to be an artificial frontier, the location was not a difficult choice. There are two places in north Britain where cross-country communication is possible. The Forth-Clyde isthmus is the shortest, at about 40 Roman miles (60km), but to choose that would have meant reoccupation of all the Lowlands of what is now Scotland. It was clearly more practicable to use the Tyne-Solway isthmus (80 Roman miles, 120km), about 140km (90 miles) further south. There was also a natural barrier in the central part of the line, the Whin Sill, which has vertical cliffs up to 33m (100ft) high in places. Although the line is not uncrossable, there being numerous gaps through the crags, the Sill does provide an obvious line to follow for about 12 miles, from MC34 to just east of MC46 near Carvoran.

Hadrian's Wall was never a rigid frontier. The fact that at least three forts on the Wall, Haltonchesters, Chesters, and Greatchesters, were supplied by aqueducts from the north, shows that Roman control did not stop at the line of the barrier. There were also outpost forts in the west some 16km (10 miles) in advance of the Wall, at Bewcastle, Netherby, and Birrens. These forts will have been used for patrols as well as static bases, further extending the limit of Roman control and influence.

Hadrian's Wall can be seen to fit into the general pattern of Roman frontiers as a line which marked the limit of formal control of the empire. However, the people living beyond it would have been subject to varying degrees of control, depending on the particular political conditions of the moment and the nearness to an outpost fort or Roman patrol. It was unlikely ever to have been seen as a fixed military frontier to be defended against intruders and a point beyond which the Romans had no control or influence.

Every frontier in the empire was built to a different design and perhaps intended for different purposes. What marks out Hadrian's Wall from other frontiers is the scale of the works, something which may have been influenced by its comparatively short length. Its design was on a monumental scale with an unusually thick curtain wall and an endless repetition of grand gateways and substantial towers, with a unity of design from end to end.

The following chapters review all aspects of how the stone Wall was built.

2

THE PLAN, AND THE START OF WORK

In its initial form the new barrier was to consist of a stone wall 10 Roman feet (hereafter Rf) wide from the River Tyne to the River Irthing and a turf wall from the Irthing to the Solway, with a ditch fronting the whole length except where cliffs made this unnecessary, and with gateways at intervals of 1 Roman mile. These gateways were protected by diminutive fortlets known as milecastles (MC), and are numbered from a theoretical one at Wallsend on the Tyne, MC0, to the western end at MC80 just west of Bowness on Solway. Between each pair of milecastles were two equi-spaced towers, known as turrets (T), taking their number from the milecastle to the east and lettered a and b. All milecastles and turrets also have names, but the numbers are very useful in indicating where on the line a site lies. One known extra tower was added subsequently at Peel Gap, between T39a and T39b. To the west of Bowness, the system of milefortlets (MF) and towers (T) extended down the coast (known as the Cumberland Coast) but without a connecting wall. The numbering of milefortlets and towers begins at MF1 to the west of Bowness.

In the original scheme the curtain wall, milecastles, and turrets were of stone as far west as the River Irthing. On the Turf Wall and down the Cumberland Coast, the milecastle/milefortlet walls had turf ramparts and timber gateways, with stone used only for the turrets/towers.

The milecastles and curtain wall on the Turf Wall were later rebuilt in stone but the milefortlets on the Cumberland Coast were not. The original milecastles on the Turf Wall have the suffix TW, while the rebuilt ones have the suffix SW. For example, MC50TW was the turf and timber predecessor to the later MC50SW.

The provision of milecastles and turrets was made regardless of the topography; they occurred with the same frequency in the undulating ground on the east, over the crags in the centre, and along the foreshore of the Solway Firth. Gateways were built even where adequate access to the north was difficult or impossible.

At an early date in the construction, a decision was taken to add forts to the line of the Wall and to provide a large, flat-bottomed ditch, now known as the Vallum, to the south. From the later second century onwards most of the turrets were abandoned, the north gateways in some milecastles were narrowed or eliminated, and the Vallum was filled in where its presence was inconvenient. Hadrian's Wall was adapted from its initial rigidity to the circumstances on the ground. This seems to emphasise that the original concept was imposed on the army by the emperor rather than developed by those working in the province.

The Wall was not completed as planned, for the width was reduced at what was probably a very early point in the building programme. The original Wall is known as the Broad Wall and the reduced Wall, typically 8Rf, as the Narrow Wall. From MC49 to MC54 the Turf Wall was replaced late in Hadrian's reign by a narrow stone wall on a slightly different line. The rest of the Turf Wall from MC54 to MC80 was rebuilt in stone at an uncertain date later in the second century. References below to the dimensions and aspect of structures assume that 'North' is the side facing the outer or enemy side of the Wall or fort and the other cardinal points take their position from this theoretical aspect.

It has long been accepted that the Wall originally terminated at Newcastle and was extended to Wallsend when forts were added to the line. The author is not convinced of this, and in the following pages the Wall is assumed to have been planned from Wallsend at the start – but readers should bear in mind that an original terminus at Newcastle is possible.

THE DETAILED DESIGN OF THE WALL AND ITS COMPONENTS

There are variations in the form of the curtain-wall footings, three designs of milecastle gateways, and three ground plans of turrets (2). The inference is that the three legions were handed an outline scheme calling for gateways and towers, and left to get on with the work in their own way.

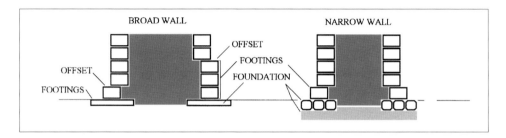

2 Foundations and footings

In a legion it was the *praefectus castrorum* who was responsible for building works. It will have been his office which prepared plans and specifications, and he would have had oversight of major projects. The detailed design of the Wall would thus have been the responsibility of the *praefectus castrorum* of each legion, the legions apparently working quite independently in this respect within the overall plan.

BROAD WALL FOUNDATIONS

The Broad Wall foundation, at almost all points where it has been investigated, consisted at most of a very shallow trench in which were laid rough slabs bedded in clay or earth with the centre filled with rubble or whin boulders and sometimes covered with a layer of clay. In some places small, rough boulders are used instead of flags. The Broad Wall between Newcastle and the Irthing is on a foundation which generally varies in width from 10.3-12.2Rf.

NARROW WALL FOUNDATIONS

From Wallsend to Newcastle the foundations consisted of a trench filled with clay and roughly quarried sandstone fragments, with water-worn boulders, usually 8.3-8.8Rf wide. Between Newcastle and the River Irthing the Narrow Wall was almost entirely built on the broad foundation.

From the Irthing to MC54 the foundations consisted of a trench of varying depth filled with clay and cobbles or other stone, with flags at ground level. The width of foundation varies from 9-9.53Rf.

INTERMEDIATE WALL FOUNDATIONS

The foundations of the Wall from MC54 to the Solway, usually known as the Intermediate Wall, are the same as those east of MC54, with a width generally of 8.9-9.8Rf. There are some variations, probably for localised structural reasons near MC65 where the width rises to 10.8Rf.

FOOTINGS

On top of the foundation slabs the first few courses of the Broad Wall form an offset below the superstructure; these courses are the footings. They are classified as two types: Standard A with one course below the offset and Standard B with three courses below the offset. These variations appear to indicate the work of different legions; the position is summarised by Breeze and Dobson (2000). There is some lack of consistency: for example, at MC20 and close to Willowford Bridge four courses were found with no offset; the builders may at times have been working to a given height rather than considering the number of courses.

The Narrow Wall has similar footings but limited to one course. However, the Wall from the Irthing to MC54 has no offset in the wall, other than that from the edge of the foundation.

CURTAIN WALL

At the time the Wall was built it was the usual, though not inevitable, practice for forts to be surrounded by an earth rampart faced with a stone wall. The earliest in Britain seems to be the fortress at Inchtuthil (Scotland), begun in the AD 80s but never completed. The fortlet at Haltwhistle Burn and the fort at Gellygaer (Wales) are examples of stone-faced forts begun during the reign of Trajan. At the same time, stone walls were added to existing forts and fortresses, something which began somewhat earlier elsewhere in the empire. It must be remembered that the stone wall, whether newly built or renovation, was invariably built as a facing to an earth rampart which might be 15-20ft wide at the base (3).

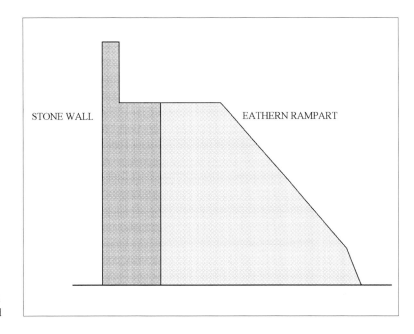

STONE WALL   EATHERN RAMPART

3 Stone fort
wall with earth
rampart behind

These walls had two faces with a rubble or earth core, varying in width between 1680mm (5ft 6in) and 915mm (3ft). The walls of the forts added to the Wall were generally about 1500mm (5ft) thick, again with an earthen rampart backing. Such evidence as is available suggests that fort walls were typically 15Rf (4440mm/14ft 7in) high. The curtain wall of the new frontier was quite unlike any of these. Not only was it designed to be 10Rf (2960mm, 9ft 7in) thick but it had no earthen rampart behind it. In practice the typical width is around 9.5Rf (2820mm, 9ft 3in). Calculations show that the height of the Wall at MCs 48 and 37 was 15Rf, and it is generally assumed that the Broad Wall was to be this height. The Narrow Wall was usually 8Rf wide. Later rebuilding of the Wall reduced the width to about 6Rf in places, but some of the extra Narrow Wall appears to be Hadrianic in date. The height of the Narrow Wall may have been the same as the Broad Wall or it may have been lower. The Venerable Bede, presumably referring to the Narrow Wall across the river from Jarrow, gives a height of 12ft and a width of 8ft.

It has been said that the width of the curtain wall was determined by the fact that a broader wall with clay core would be more stable than a narrow one. In fact the reverse is true, and any instability in a clay-bonded core would be greater in the broader wall, simply because with the broader wall there is a greater weight of unstable core against a given area of facing stone.

The use of mortar to bond the core of the Broad Wall was once assumed to be the norm, but it is now clear that very little mortar was used. However, there are some instances where it was bonded with mortar, especially at Great Hill (east of MC12) where gunpowder had to be used to demolish the remains of the Wall during road works in 1926. It seems probable that work began in places with the use of a mortared core, especially between MCs7 and 12 but that the specification was soon changed to the use of clay.

The Broad Wall incorporated single courses of thin stone usually described as 'bonding courses'. They are very clear at MC37, Housesteads, where two of them are seen to the west of the north gate, about 1200mm (4ft) apart. They do not occur in post-Hadrianic rebuilding, and not always in the original Wall; for example, the north wall of MC48, Poltross Burn, stands over 2m (6ft) high but shows no sign of a thin course. Despite the name, their purpose is unclear. Although they tend to be longer on the face than the walling stones they are very little deeper into the wall than the stones on which they rest, as may be seen in the stretch immediately east of Birdoswald.

These courses may represent intervals in the work, and a relationship to scaffolding has been suggested. This is in fact quite impossible as the coursing of the Wall normally follows the slope of the ground and scaffolding must be built horizontally. The bonding course on the west wall of Greatchesters fort, for example, slopes at about 20° to the horizontal.

MILECASTLES AND MILEFORTLETS

With a few exceptions the area enclosed by the milecastles on the stone wall is remarkably uniform, with near-standard dimensions of 50 x 60Rf (14.8m x 17.76m/48ft 6in x 58ft 3in), although one legion had the short axis running north–south ('short axis milecastle') while the other two used the long axis ('long axis milecastle') for this dimension.

Small fortlets were usually constructed to hold a garrison of a century or so, whereas the majority of milecastles seem to have held only 8 or 12 men. MCs 47 and 48 probably held 32 men if the scale of accommodation was the same as in a normal auxiliary barrack. However, these buildings are almost certainly not the original ones, and there is some evidence that the number of buildings in milecastles increased with time.

Strictly speaking, milecastles are not in fact 'fortlets,' in the sense of being a base for sub-units. Rather, they seem simply to be protected accommodation for a handful of gate guards, a completely new departure. They were diminutive. There was only one smaller defended encampment in Britain, the tiny station at Brownhart Law, 41 x 47Rf, which was probably an outstation of the nearby Chew Green fortlet just across the modern border of Scotland.

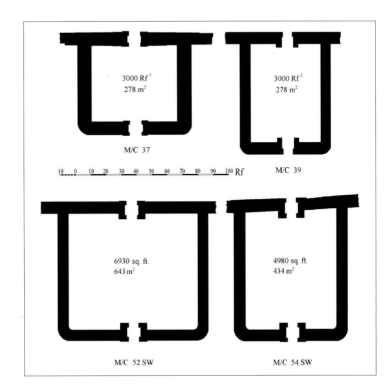

4 Comparative plans: Stone wall and south-west milecastles

The design of diminutive 'standard' milecastles did not survive into the Antonine frontier. The majority of the seven fortlets on the Antonine Wall, of which the size is reasonably securely known, are larger although still very small by the standards of fortlets elsewhere.

Stone milecastle walls are structurally and dimensionally very similar to the curtain wall, with the exception that the core was normally, though not invariably, bonded with mortar rather than clay. Even without an inner rampart, a stone wall some 2.9m (9ft 6in) wide around a very small enclosure is remarkable.

There are exceptions to the general uniformity of size. The western two milecastles on the Stone Wall, MCs 47 and 48, just short of the River Irthing, are noticeably larger than the standard, at 390m² (4200Rf²). Across the river, MCs 52SW and 54SW are the largest milecastles known (4).

On the Cumberland Coast, apart from an atypical small fort at Cardurnock, MF5, there are only three or four milefortlets for which reasonably firm dimensions are known. MF20 was probably designed to 'standard' milecastle size, as was MF21, while MF22 was designed to be the size of MC48. MF1 may have been very slightly larger than a 'standard' milecastle.

MILECASTLE GATEWAYS

Each legion produced its own plan for the gateways (5). There was a single-portal gate in both north and south walls, consisting of a substantial arch at each end of the gate passage, carried on piers of large, squared stones. It is highly likely that there was a tower over the north gate to maintain the sequence of elevated lookout points between each pair of turrets and probably one over the south gate as well. In some milecastles, the passage walls were of stones much more carefully squared than those of the curtain wall. The outer arch on each gate was closed by heavy wooden doors.

It used to be clear which legion built which type of gate, tower, and Standard A or B curtain wall. However, there is now some doubt about their identity, and Breeze and Dobson (2000) use the letters A, B, C when allocating legions to these structures. The design of the three types of gateway and their occurrence in relation to the axes is sufficiently consistent to accept an allocation to legions A, B, and C, even though it is not entirely certain which legion is which. Reference to the gate types as I, II/IV, and III is a long-established tradition.

Type I – legion A
Type I has the same length as the width of Broad Wall, plus a projection of 50-70mm (2-3in) on each face as a form of emphasis. Where the milecastle wall is

less than 10Rf wide the gate projected into the milecastle, as exemplified by the south gate of MC42, where the projection is between 170mm and 390mm (6.5 and 15in). The south wall is only 2540mm (8ft 4in) rather than the average Broad Wall of 2820mm (9ft 3in).

The reason for the consistency of the length of type I gateways is that space has to be given for the doors to open, and the projecting inner respond would prevent this if the length of the gate were reduced. The south gate of MC42 comes very close to this, as the foundation blocks for the inner piers had to be cut away to give clearance to the doors.

Type II/IV – legion C

These gates have no projecting responds on the inner ends of the gate passage but have instead flush piers. They are the same length as the thickness of the Broad Wall (type IV), but where they occur in Narrow Wall milecastles the inner ends project into the milecastle (type II). This projection is probably due to the need to maintain a reasonable depth to the towers over the gateways.

As there are no projecting responds on the inner side of the gate, the arch must have been of greater span than that on the outer side, unless the tower were carried by a lintel. The same design feature appears in the gateways of Housesteads fort and will have given problems to the builders, something which is discussed in chapter 8.

Type III – legion B

These gateways have projecting inner and outer responds, but this type always projects into the

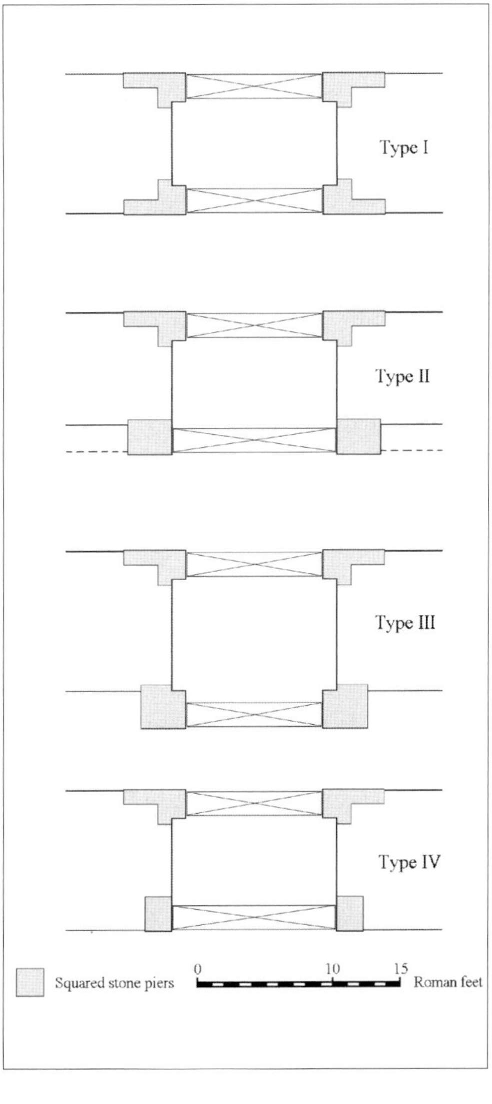

Type I

Type II

Type III

Type IV

Squared stone piers   0   10   15   Roman feet

5 The four types of milecastle gateways

27

milecastle, regardless of whether the walls are broad or narrow gauge, with a length of around 3900mm (12ft 9in). MCs 19, 20, and 22 have very short inner projections and could be a variant of Type I, but without re-excavation they cannot be reclassified. The only reason which the author can find for this design is a desire to have a greater floor area to the tower over the gates. The identical plans shown by north and south gates of type III point very strongly to there having been a tower over both gateways.

THE PURPOSE OF THE MILECASTLES

The fact that MC37, Housesteads, only some 400m west of the fort, was provided with a barrack block whereas the third-century Knag Burn gateway, 100m east of the fort, had no accommodation and must have been manned from the fort, suggests that the milecastles had a different, or additional, function to that of merely guarding a gateway. Patrolling to the north is unlikely given a force of only 8 or 12. Only the few larger milecastles around the Irthing could have carried out patrols, especially if they contained a small element of cavalry for which there is space. The fact that four items of horse equipment were found at MC48 may point to the existence of cavalry in the garrison there. In theory, MC52sw, the largest, had room for perhaps 32 infantry and 12 cavalry (6), although there is no evidence for the internal buildings. There is much work needed on the purpose of milecastles.

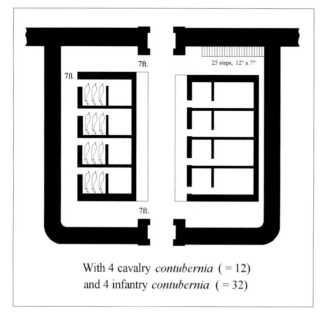

With 4 cavalry *contubernia* (= 12)
and 4 infantry *contubernia* (= 32)

6 Milecastle 52sw, conjectural internal buildings

TURRETS

Turrets were in general terms around 3660 x 3960mm internally (12 x 13ft), perhaps 10.7m (35ft) to the eaves, with a ground floor entrance; there may have been a balcony at second floor level. The internal area, on two floors, has been calculated as around 29m² (300 sq.ft). The roof may have been either flat or pitched, this author strongly favouring the latter. Depending on the legion responsible for building them, turrets have their entrances at either the east or west of the south wall, with side and south walls either 900mm or 1200mm (3ft or 4ft) thick. Turrets are recessed into the curtain wall normally leaving the north wall about 1500mm (5ft) thick, but there are exceptions to this: Ts41a, 44b, 45a, 48a and 48b have narrow north walls.

The Mains Rigg tower, Robin Hood's Butt on the Maiden Way, and the Birdoswald tower, of probably Trajanic date, resemble the turrets in size and wall thickness but with the doorway at first floor level, appropriate for an isolated tower and a feature which is common in German examples. The tower at Pike Hill, on the Wall but not in the sequence of Wall turrets, is a similar size but with a ground floor doorway.

When the details of the new Wall were considered, this design was an obvious one to use. The alterations needed for the turrets to form part of the new running barrier were the insertion of a ground floor doorway, probably ground floor windows, and provision for bonding with the curtain wall. This last was a completely new element in watch towers, but would have been familiar to the builders of fort interval towers. No other major alterations to the plan would be needed, although staircases were provided in at least some turrets.

FORTS

At an early point in the building programme the decision was taken to add forts to the line of the Wall. There were seven new forts on the stone wall: Wallsend, Benwell, Rudchester, Halton Chesters, Chesters, Housesteads, and Greatchesters; all but Housesteads and Greatchesters projected north of the Wall (7). On the turf wall there were five new forts: Birdoswald, Castlesteads, Stanwix, Burgh-by-Sands, and Bowness. The Cumberland Coast had three certain Hadrianic forts, at Beckfoot, Maryport, and Moresby.

On present evidence, Newcastle is post-Hadrianic, Carrawburgh dates to the 130s, Drumburgh may be a later addition, and Vindolanda and Carvoran were existing Stanegate forts.

As already noted, fort walls were significantly thinner than the curtain wall, and the interval towers around the fort walls were smaller in area and had thinner walls than the turrets.

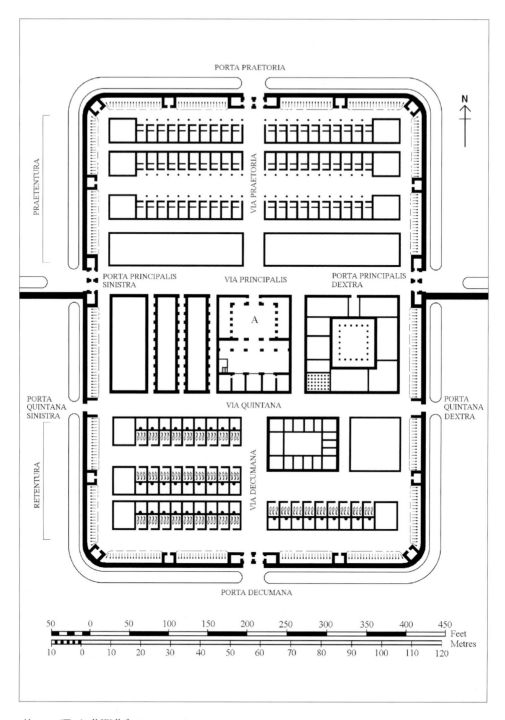

Above: 7 'Typical' Wall fort

Opposite: 8 Rebuilt gateway at South Shields

The gateways were normally of twin-portal design, that is with two openings side by side. The exceptions are the extra side gates (*porta quintana sinistra, porta quintana dextra*) provided in those forts where the main side gates were north of the wall.

The piers of the gateways were similar to milecastle gateways, with the addition of a central *spina* to support the inner ends of the two arches. The major difference between the milecastle and fort gateways lies in the superstructure. Whereas the former have small, simple towers, the latter have substantial upper storeys, with towers at either side and probably some superstructure above the portals as exemplified by the reconstruction at South Shields (*8*).

MATERIALS USED IN BUILDING THE WALL

Frontier works show considerable variation in materials. In Upper Germany there was a palisade of contiguous wooden posts, up to 305mm (1ft) diameter, and in Raetia (roughly modern Switzerland) a stone wall about a metre wide was used. In Africa, the *Fossatum* varied between dry-stone walls, and dressed and mortared stone. The *limes Porolissensis* was part earthwork and part narrow stone wall, while in Britain five-eighths of the wall of Hadrian was in stone and the remainder in turf. The later Antonine Wall was of turf or clay on a cobble base. There was clearly no over-riding policy on the design of linear barriers; they were built in the most appropriate materials for the locality.

RENDER AND LIMEWASH

In recent years it has been suggested that the curtain wall was either limewashed or rendered, or both. 'Limewashing' is painting with a thin coat of slaked lime, and 'rendering' is to cover with a coating of mortar to give a more or less smooth surface.

There are a number of reasons for coating the surface of a wall. Limewashing can have a protective effect, reducing the erosion of mortar in the joints and keeping the weather from the surface of the stonework. This last is only really useful where the nature of the stone means that it is subject to rapid weathering, something which does not apply to the Wall east of the Irthing. To serve such a purpose the limewash has to be renewed at regular intervals. Limewash would also have a dramatic effect, emphasising the monumental nature of the work as a symbol of power.

Rendering also has a protective effect, but is more usually applied in conjunction with scribed or painted joint lines, to give the false appearance of ashlar. It is debatable whether the local inhabitants would have been more impressed by false ashlar than by squared rubble, but it was certainly a common feature of Roman architecture as was whitewashing. Some such finish is to be expected on the walls of internal buildings of forts and milecastles, and perhaps on their outer walls also. This could also extend to turrets, although there is no convincing evidence for any external finish applied to any part of the Wall.

Excavations in Peel Gap in 1986-88 revealed a stone from the string course, about two thirds of which was covered by lime, and this has been taken as an indication of the use of whitewash. However, rain falling on fresh mortar causes leaching out of the lime, producing a very white coating which sets hard on the surface of the stones below. Indeed, after consolidation work in 1996, on the east side of the tower in Peel Gap several stones were partly covered by a thick layer of lime which in isolation could be mistaken for limewash (9). In view of this, a few part-whitened stones cannot be evidence for the deliberate limewashing of the Wall.

Excavations at Denton, where the Newcastle Western By-pass crosses the Wall, have revealed other evidence of how the Wall surface was treated. When the fallen wall was robbed of its stones the pattern of joints was left as quite large pieces of white mortar. The mortar seems to have been applied to the joints with a trowel in a manner which left mortar smeared liberally over the faces of the stones at either side of the joints. This was the usual method of pointing rubble work until recent years, and excavations at Birdoswald revealed original pointing on the south *horrea* which parallels the repointing at Denton.

9 Lime from consolidation mortar leached out over facing stones (Peel Gap, 1996)

The preservation of hard white mortar on the south face of the Wall at Heddon-on-the-Wall has been taken as evidence of rendering. There certainly are small areas of mortar on the stones (the largest dimension is 10-12mm), but they occur on the lower few courses where mortar splashes are to be expected. Not only does mortar fall from above during the building or repointing of any wall, but mixing of mortar at the foot of a new or existing wall can result in major areas of what could after many years be taken for the remains of render (*10*).

The amount of mortar needed to render the curtain wall can easily be calculated. If it is assumed that the faces project by up to 25mm, and that the render would barely cover the high spots, then to cover both sides of the original 49 miles of stone curtain wall 11555m^3 (15,112 cu.yds) of mortar would be needed. No allowance has been made for wastage and, as the projection of the faces allowed for is low, quantities are likely to have been significantly higher.

Evidence of rendering has survived on watch towers in Germany, and inside a guardroom of the south gate at Chesters. It is surprising that, if it existed, it has not survived on Hadrian's Wall. It might be expected that stones at the foot of the Wall, buried by detritus and fallen masonry, would preserve clear evidence of limewash, but such a find has not been made. Until a considerable number of stones limewashed or rendered over the entirety of the faces are found, the evidence cannot be regarded as satisfactory.

10 Mortar splashes on a modern brick wall giving the effect of render

THE DITCH

On the north side of the curtain wall was a large ditch. At the best-preserved sections at Haltonchesters, Chesters, and Birdoswald, the original dimensions appear to have been 8230mm wide by 2745mm deep (27ft x 9ft), with a standard military V-shaped section, although there are wide variations in these figures elsewhere. The berm (the flat area between Wall and ditch) is normally about 6m (20ft) wide.

Excavations at Black Carts showed that the ditch, cut through whin bedrock, is only 3500m wide by 800mm deep (11ft 6in x 2ft 8in). About 1 mile to the west, close to the site of MC30, the unfinished section at Limestone Corner is about 4270mm wide x 2440mm deep (14ft x 8ft). The width is reasonably consistent and was perhaps intended to be the finished size, although it has vertical instead of sloping sides probably due to the strong vertical jointing of the whinstone. Immediately to the west of this section the ditch was never dug to full depth and appears now as a shallow depression. Given that the ditch of the Vallum at Limestone Corner was completed, it is most unlikely that the legionaries were defeated by the hardness of the rock.

There are a number of other points where the ditch was unfinished where there is no reason why it could not have been taken to full depth; it seems more probable that a policy change was responsible for all uncompleted sections of ditch.

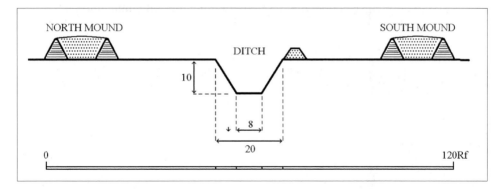

11 Typical cross-section of the Vallum

The ditch is not continuous, as it is omitted where the crags, or the foreshore of the Solway, made it redundant. In broad terms it is present from Wallsend to MC34, MC38-38a, Peel Gap to MC40, T42a-T43b, T45b-MC73 (apart from the section facing the River Eden), with some very short sections along the crags amounting to a few hundred yards. The total length is about 65 Roman miles, or 96km (60 miles).

A series of holes (*cippi*) has been found on the berm at Wallsend and Throckley. They are in three rows and are believed to have held some form of obstruction such as tree branches. No sign of similar features was found in the 1999 excavations of the berm at Black Carts and Appletree. Their precise purpose and extent is uncertain.

THE VALLUM

The earthworks to the south of the Wall, incorrectly named by Bede (1, 5) as the Vallum, are unlike frontier works anywhere else in the empire. They consist of a ditch flanked by wide berms with the upcast built up into mounds set back to either side; there is often a third mound on the southern lip of the ditch (*11*).

The ditch is not of the standard military type, but is flat bottomed, typically 6100mm (20ft) wide at the top, 2440mm (8ft) wide at the base, and 3050mm (10ft) deep. As with the Wall ditch, there are considerable variations from these typical dimensions. The north and south mounds, separated from the ditch by berms 9145mm (30ft) wide, are typically 6100mm (20ft) wide at the base. The original height does not survive, but if all material from the ditch were used in building these mounds, and the sides were at 60°, they may have been 1525mm (5ft) high and 4270mm (14ft) wide across the top.

The lesser south mound – 'marginal mound' – appears on the south lip of the ditch at a number of places and has generally been regarded as the product of cleaning out the ditch. However, recent excavations at Black Carts and Appletree indicate that the marginal mound was built on the same cleared ground surface as the main south mound. But in other places, the marginal mound is composed of peaty and silty material which would seem to be derived from maintenance of the ditch.

A significant point about the Vallum is that the ditch is always present, while the Wall ditch is intermittent or not fully dug. Clearly, for the Vallum the ditch was the significant feature. It ran from the River Tyne, adjacent to MC4, to Bowness without interruption, a length of 76 Roman miles or 112km (70 miles).

THE START OF WORK

Once the form of the Wall had been decided upon, the task was to set the general line of the new frontier. One may imagine the choice being made by a party of senior officers, with or without the emperor, riding slowly across the countryside, covering perhaps 10 miles a day, accompanied by a working party to erect small cairns or posts at intervals; a matter of a week or so to cover the isthmus. Given that the new frontier was to be on the Tyne-Solway, the line was in a sense limited by the topography. The edge of the crags on the central sector was the obvious line to take, and it remained only for the two ends of this part to be joined to the estuaries of Tyne and Solway. It may well have been unnecessary for senior officers to do more than take a general look at the line on a map. Maps seem to have been commonly available in the Roman army (Sherk 1974). It then remained for the precise line to be determined.

Surveying
The detailed survey work would have been carried out by legionary surveyors (*mensores*). There were probably 10 *mensores* to a legion, or 30 available in the three legions in Britain.

Very sophisticated surveying would not have been necessary; unlike a road or an aqueduct the Wall did not have to have great regard for the contours beneath it but might be expected to take account of those to the north. In practice the Wall made no great effort to take the line with the best outlook. There are a number of points at which the view to the north is limited by rising ground, when a better line was available. But selecting the line with the best view would only have been of real significance if the line formed the absolute limit of Roman observation, which it did not.

The surveyors worked in a series of straight sections in the east and west, and in the central sector the line was fixed by the edge of the Whin Sill, whose turns were normally followed closely. In the eastern sector the Wall clearly makes changes of direction on local high points, notably adjacent to MCs 10, 12, 14, 16, 30, and T20a, and still visible when driving on the Military Road. However, changes of direction were made at other points. Between T25b and MC26 a 30° northwards turn is made on a false crest some way to the west of the true summit. It looks as though the surveyors were working eastwards from the site of the bridge at Chesters, sighting up to the visible edge of the hillside, even though this was not the top of the slope. From this point the Wall runs straight to Chesters fort, and then makes a turn of 2-3° to the north to run straight to its most northerly point at Limestone Corner, where it turns southwards again to aim for the start of the crags of the Whin Sill.

The Whin Sill is followed because it is there. There was little consideration given to either the steepness of the slopes along the line or to access from front and rear in respect of access for heavy materials and for ease of building.

Recent work by Hargreaves on the surveying of the Wall has confirmed that Roman linear constructions were set out using the *groma*, in a series of straight alignments. On the Wall he has found that these alignments vary from 3090m (3379yds) to 1m. For the short alignments cords were probably used in place of the *groma*.

Curves were few; one which is visible today is on the west side of Sycamore Gap (just east of MC39, Castle Nick). There is a very interesting turn to the west of MC42. Near the top of the hill, about 20m short of the quarry face, the Wall turns north through about 80°; the south, or outer, face makes a tight curve while the inner face shows a sharp angle, in the same way as the southern corners of the Hadrianic milecastles.

There were two separate operations to be carried out: surveying the precise line and measuring the positions for milecastles and turrets. The speed with which the precise line could have been marked out will have depended on the degree of urgency in the orders, but if necessary it could have been completed within four or five weeks.

It has been argued that access to the Wall line was initially from Dere Street and Carlisle, from which points the line might be surveyed to the Tyne and the Solway. At the same time, separate parties could have worked to the east and west ends of the Whin Sill. There were three additional fixed points from where survey had to be conducted: the crossing of the North Tyne at Chesters, of the Irthing at Willowford, and the Eden at Carlisle. To the east of Newcastle, the crossing of the Ouseburn, and perhaps the Lort Burn, may also have been fixed points. In the central sector, the Wall simply stays as close as possible to the edge of the Whin Sill, which meant that any number of parties could have been at work there with little risk of the lines failing to join up.

The approximate lengths of each section (in Wall-miles) are as follows: Wallsend to Ouseburn 3 miles; Ouseburn to Dere Street 18 miles; Dere Street to North Tyne 5 miles; North Tyne to the eastern end of Whin Sill (MC34) 7 miles; Whin Sill 13 miles; Western end of Whin Sill (say MC46) to Irthing 3 miles; Irthing to the Eden 17 miles; Eden to Bowness 14 miles.

Given that the general line had been roughly marked out and the river crossing points selected, the final surveying could have been carried out from both ends of each section. The maximum length for one party to survey would thus be nine Wall-miles, with 16 survey parties at work at once. At a rate of, say, one hour to a quarter mile, and given a six-hour day (to allow for returning to base), the longest section would be complete in six days, and the other sections within that time. An extra day at the junction of each of the sections to allow for any realignment would bring the total to a maximum of 13 days.

Measuring the location of the turrets and milecastles would ideally have been carried out from one end of the Wall, and at a rate of, say, only 5 miles a day would take 16 days. Including the initial survey of the general line, the whole work could have been completed in about a month.

3

QUARRYING AND WORKING STONE

Comparatively little is known about the organisation of quarrying for ordinary building stone in Roman times. Rather more is known about the methods of quarrying although, because of the better survival of quarries, most of the research relates to the continental provinces. Few quarries in Britain are of certain Roman date, and fewer still provide evidence of the methods employed.

OVERVIEW OF THE STONE AND QUARRIES

The stones generally used for building the Wall are sandstone and gritstone. Broadly speaking, gritstone consists of angular grains, often wind-blown, while sandstone has more rounded grains, often water-borne and thus becoming more abraded. Gritstone tends to have coarser grain sizes.

The nature of the stone varies along the line of the Wall according to the quarry from which it came; some is easy to work, some is next to impossible. The hardness of stone is not necessarily related to its durability. There does not appear to be any evidence that the selection of stone was based upon anything but its proximity to the Wall line; this is logical as it reduces transport problems. For example, at MC48 the intractable contact-metamorphosed sandstone from the adjacent valley of the Poltross Burn has been used in preference to the much more suitable and more easily worked stone used at Birdoswald, which appears to have been quarried from Coombe Crag, about 2.5 miles from the fort and 4 miles from MC48. As a result the north gate of the latter is probably the worst-finished piece of work on the Wall. Only the dolerite from the Whin Sill was largely ignored for facing stones owing to its extreme hardness and difficulty of working. It was, however, widely used in the central sector for the foundations and for core stone.

The weight of stone to be transported was a major problem faced by the Wall builders. As a guide, stone from the Black Pasture Quarry, which was used to build the bridge over the North Tyne at Chesters, weighs 2325kg/m^3 or 145lb per cubic foot.

For practical purposes, nothing whatsoever is known about the organisation of quarrying for the Wall although a great deal can be deduced. It can be assumed that quarry operations were carried out with the ultimate use of the blocks in mind, but we do not know whether, as one might logically expect, lists of cutting sizes were sent to the quarries. There is no reason why this could not have been done, and there is certainly evidence from Rome of the detailed full size setting-out of significant architectural features which would make this possible (see Haselberger 1985, 1994 and 1995).

In the central sector there are still ample traces of small quarries to be seen within half a mile of the Wall, both north and south, presumably many of them Roman although they are impossible to date without inscriptions which few of them carry. Toolmarks are, of themselves, undateable as basic stone-quarrying techniques varied little from antiquity to the mid-twentieth century.

Immediately to the west of Haltwhistle Burn fortlet is a quarry which carried an inscription of legion VI (*RIB* 1680) until it was removed by modern quarrying. As this legion is believed to have arrived in the province in AD 122, the quarry was probably used, or reopened, to supply the Wall builders. When a quarry on Barcombe Hill above Chesterholm was reopened in 1837 an arm-purse was discovered, holding coins current in the early years of Hadrian's reign. Fallowfield Fell quarry, to the east of Chesters, had an inscription, now removed to Chesters museum for safety, cut by Flavius Carantinus (*RIB* 1442); the date of the inscription is unknown. The sandstone quarry at Queen's Crags, north of Housesteads, bears an undated Roman inscription. To the west of Birdoswald further Roman quarries are identified by inscriptions, none of which are closely dateable: Coombe Crag (*RIB* 1946-52), Lodge Crag (*RIB* 1953-54), and a group of quarries in Cumbria (*RIB* 998-1016).

The proximity of the quarries to the Wall suggests that they were used, and presumably specifically opened, for its building. Much of the Wall was probably built from small quarries opened all along the line, wherever reasonable stone could be found near enough to keep transport to a minimum.

It has been argued that the ditch of the Wall was used, in one area at least, to provide all the materials used in building the Wall, but the wastage involved in quarrying building stone from such a small excavation makes this improbable. It is virtually certain that the builders would have made use of any stone from the ditch to fill the core, but the use of the ditch to provide more than a small percentage of the facing stones is unlikely.

Types of walling

Before discussing the methods employed in quarrying it will be useful to establish definitions of types of walling stone used as an aid to understanding the nature of the requirements for the quarryman (*12*).

The curtain wall, the walls around the forts and milecastles, and the turrets, are mostly built of *squared rubble*. The stones are more or less roughly squared up, with wide joints. They are generally worked to something of a taper, as this both increases the hold of the mortar and makes accuracy in working less important. The faces are most often hammer finished or natural and tend to be rather lumpy and rounded.

In places the facing stones deteriorate to *coursed rubble*, that is stone straight from the thin beds in the quarry, laid in rough courses; this can be seen in parts of MC48, Poltross Burn, and on the stretch of curtain wall running down towards Willowford bridge immediately west of T48b.

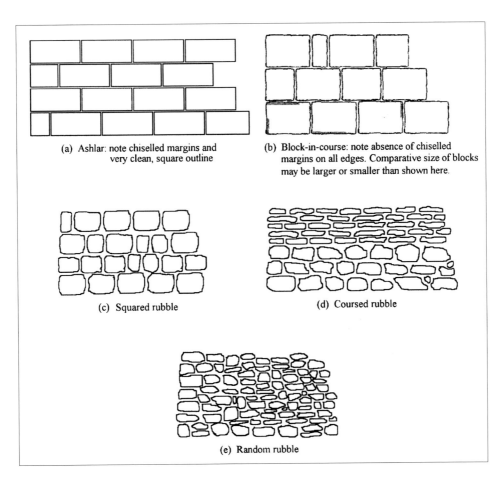

(a) Ashlar: note chiselled margins and very clean, square outline

(b) Block-in-course: note absence of chiselled margins on all edges. Comparative size of blocks may be larger or smaller than shown here.

(c) Squared rubble

(d) Coursed rubble

(e) Random rubble

12 Types of walling

The term 'rubble' should not in any way be taken as a derogatory term. Squared-rubble wall construction is simple, relatively cheap, makes an adequate and reasonably durable job, and does not call for a high degree of skill either in preparation of the stones or in building. For a structurally simple building of whatever size there is no real need to put in any greater effort, and the Roman army did not do so when building Hadrian's Wall. The techniques used in quarrying for rubble can be, as will be shown, very simple indeed.

The Wall is sometimes described as being built of 'ashlar'. This is a common misapprehension, and ashlar is in fact very rare on the Wall. By definition, *ashlar* has carefully worked beds and joints, with fine joints generally no more than 3-4mm (1/8-3/16in), and set in horizontal courses. By its nature, ashlar must be quarried from solid beds of stone.

The other type of stone encountered on the Wall is that which is suitable for dressing to specific profiles, such as the piers and voussoirs of the milecastle and fort gateways, and the various decorative pieces. This is usually referred to by the generic name of *dimension stone*; the term refers to the need for large blocks which can be worked to specific dimensions rather than to the style of building.

Occasionally another class of building will be seen, where the blocks are somewhere between ashlar and squared rubble, and known as *block-in-course*. This is an old-fashioned but convenient term to describe the large blocks of masonry seen in Victorian dock and railway engineering; it has much in common with Roman gate piers. The blocks are squared and brought to fair joints, and the faces usually either rock-faced or punched. Chiselled margins might be expected on the quoins but not elsewhere. Massive solidity rather than sophistication is the keynote of this class of work.

Methods of quarrying

Where the stone occurs in relatively thin beds, perhaps 100-500mm thick, it can often be extracted with the use of crowbars to lever the slabs out, and heavy hammers to break them into easily handled pieces. In modern times a 'bursting' hammer (*13*) of up to 28lb weight with one flat face about 3in square and one face shaped to a wedge with the axis parallel to the axis of the shaft has been used.

No certain examples of such a tool have survived from Roman times, but in the same pit which contained the altars of Marcus Cocceius Firmus (*RIB* 2174-2178) at Auchendavy were found two large iron hammers. Their function is not known, but they are described as having 'been much used, for their faces are greatly battered.' They are almost exactly the same weight as the modern bursting hammer and are probably Roman examples of this tool.

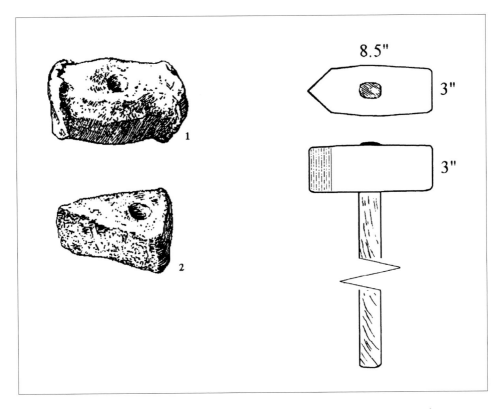

13 Roman bursting hammer (1), Roman splitting hammer (2) *after Behn*; modern splitting hammer

The joints of the facing stones on the Wall sometimes exhibit signs of having been split by the wedge face of a bursting hammer, or a splitting hammer, or by a large wedge struck by a heavy hammer, to produce a clean fracture.

Once the slabs are broken into manageable pieces with the bursting hammer, minor dressing may be carried out to knock off any particularly awkward angles. The Roman walling hammers shown in *figure 14* are ideal for this purpose. The appearance of the finished work depends very much on the regularity of the beds. The thinner beds will usually give a random or coursed rubble, but the thicker beds will, with some more or less rough dressing, produce the squared rubble typical of the Wall.

Where the stone occurs in continuous deep beds the method of extraction becomes rather more technical, and the stone has to be split by the use of wedges (15). It may be possible to utilise existing open cracks, but it is usually necessary to use a hammer and punch to cut holes to take the wedges. The holes are cut to a rough taper matching that of the wedge, and sufficiently deep to allow the wedge to be driven to its full extent without hitting the bottom.

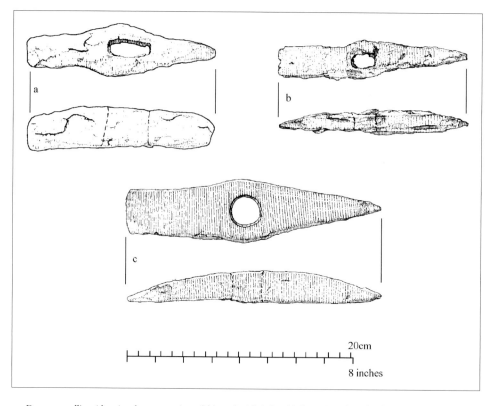

14 Roman walling/dressing hammers (a and b), and pick/adze (c) from Northumberland, *after Manning*

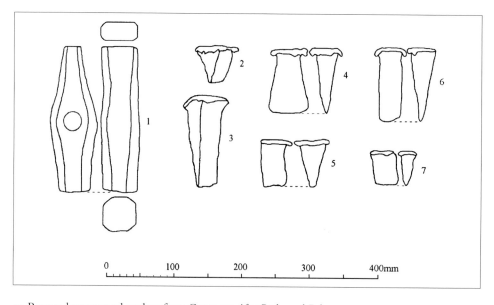

15 Roman hammer and wedges from Germany. *After Röder and Behn*

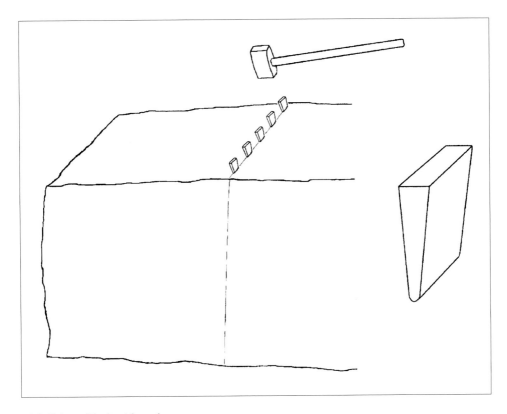

16 Splitting a block with wedges

A series of holes is cut in a straight line on the top bed of the stone along the desired line of fracture. Depending on the particular nature of the stone the wedges may need to be continued, in the same plane, down one or more sides.

Wedges are normally much wider than they are thick, a form which encourages splitting along the predetermined line. One is inserted in each hole and driven home with a heavy hammer in repeated sequence (*16*). When the tension in the stone becomes too great, a crack will form in the plane of the wedges, and the stone will split away to give a surprisingly regular surface. In order to increase the accuracy of the break, a shallow groove is sometimes cut along the intended plane of fracture.

Early twentieth-century quarrying sometimes made use of a continuous slot into which the wedges were inserted, a practice well-known to Roman quarrymen and identified by the author on the Roman quarry face at Pigeon Clint, on the River Irthing about 50m west of the quarry inscription *RIB* 1016. Slots at Fallowfield Fell may well be Roman, although in the light of modern quarrying there this is uncertain.

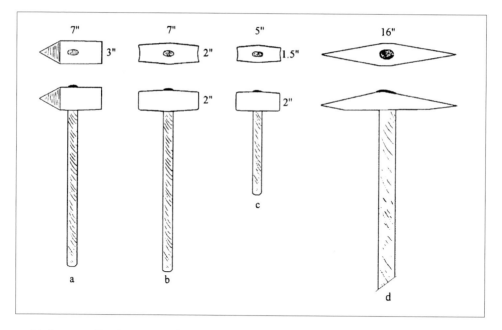

17 Modern scappling hammers and pick

Some wedge holes are found many metres below the top of the quarry face. They cannot have been intended to split the stone, as this would have meant lifting several hundred tons of rock. It may be that they are related to access to the top of the quarry faces, perhaps to secure ladders or staging.

QUARRY DRESSING

For producing dimension stone, the next stage is to achieve a roughly rectangular block in advance of detailed dressing. This operation is often referred to as scappling or scabbling. In modern times the form of tool used tends to be a heavy rectangular head drawn to a point at one end and known as a scappling hammer or kivel (*17a*). Heavy picks were also used for this purpose.

Another tool used for roughly squaring quarried blocks is the spalling hammer, which has two concave faces, each face having two cutting edges (*17b*), and comes in various sizes. As its name suggests it is used for removing large spalls or lumps of stone. Both tools are normally used two-handed although the smaller spalling hammer, usually referred to as a 'dressing hammer' (*17c*), is small enough to use in one hand. There is also the large pick (*17d*) used for roughly squaring up blocks. A Roman equivalent of a scappling hammer is shown in *figure 18*.

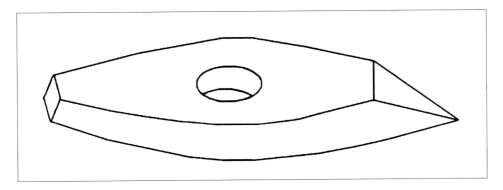

18 Roman scappling hammer. *After Blagg*

The quarried blocks may be too large for a specific piece of work, and have to be reduced into two or more smaller blocks. This can be done with small, square-section wedges, or even using ordinary punches, an operation known as 'coping'. It is also possible to saw stone, using either a toothed blade or plain blade with sand as the cutting medium depending on the type of stone. Both types of saw were known in Roman times (Pliny, *Book XXXVI*, ix; xliv; xlviii). No evidence has been found on the Wall for the use of saws.

MASONS' TOOLS

There has been little change in the hand tools over the past three or four millennia, something confirmed not only by surviving tools but by observation of the toolmarks on the stonework of the Wall. There are two basic types of tools used by the Romans, and mostly still in use today: those such as picks, walling hammers, axes, and adzes which act directly on the stone; and various types of chisel which are driven by a hammer or mallet. A number of examples from the author's tool kit are shown in *figure 19*, and may be compared with the Roman examples. It will be seen that the form of many tools has changed very little.

Large picks were used in the quarry to remove awkward projections and for rough dressing, but small picks were used for quite detailed dressing to a finished surface. Axes and adzes are used for fine dressing, and do not need to be heavy or thick-bladed. Blake (1999) illustrates an axe/adze from Vindolanda (*20*) which is only 100mm (4in) long and clearly appropriate for delicate work. *Figure 20* illustrates a Roman axe which is almost identical to the modern one seen in *figure 19f*. Axes are quite capable of producing a fine finish to ashlar, and can give an effect indistinguishable from a chiselled surface.

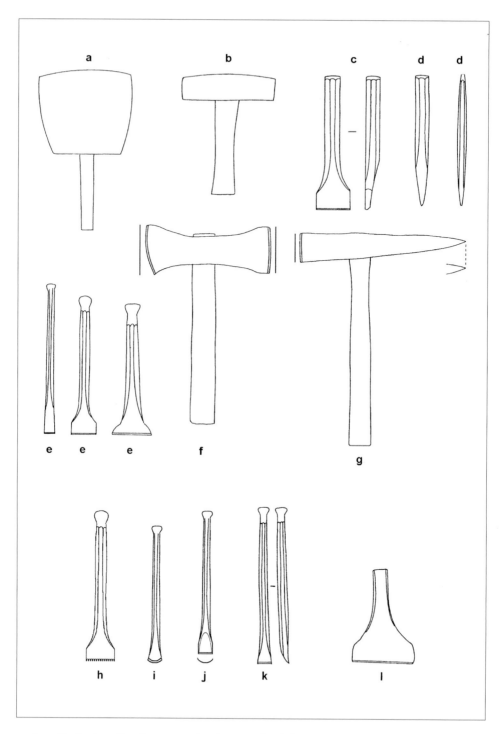

19 A small selection of modern masons' tools – a: mallet, b: hammer, c: pitcher, d: punches, e: chisels, f: axe, g: walling hammer, h: claw, i: bullnose, j: gouge, k: bent chisel, l: nicker

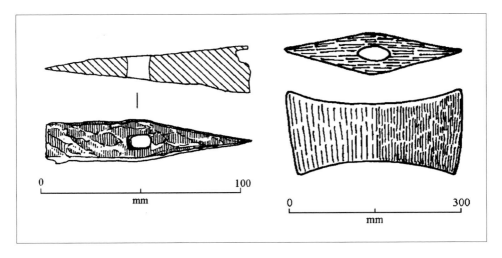

20 Roman axes. *After Blake* and *Blagg*

The chisel is a bar of steel (or iron with a steel tip), typically about 18mm (0.75in) in diameter and normally at least 150mm (6in) long; the diameter may be as little as 6mm (0.25in) for fine work. The length rarely exceeds 230-255mm (9-10in). One end is drawn out in a tapered cross-section to form the blade, the width of which varies according to the work in hand. A very wide variety of work can be carried out with no more than 12, 25, and 50mm chisels (0.5in, 1in and 2in). The body of the stone chisel may be significantly stouter than that of a wood chisel but the blade is often more finely drawn out (*21*). Most sedimentary stones are not particularly hard to work and do not necessarily call for the use of very stout chisels and heavy hammers; today, it is not uncommon for the softer limestones to be worked with wood chisels.

Chisels are today usually struck with an oval wooden mallet, although a hammer is more common when working marble and granite. The hammer used by the mason tends to be long-headed, usually around 150mm (6in), with a striking face not much more than 25mm square, and of a weight which varies from 1-2.5kg (2-5lb).

Modern chisels used with a mallet are drawn out and upset at the upper end to form a broad, shallow dome (*22a*), while those for use with a hammer have a plain end (*22b*). Tools used with a hammer tend to spread at the head, as shown in *figure 22c*, but the effect is quite different from the deliberate mallet head.

The use of a mallet in Roman times is uncertain, although highly likely; it was certainly used in Ancient Kingdom Egypt. What seems to be a very clear example of a mallet-headed chisel is shown in *figure 23*, and it does appear that not only did the Roman masons use a mallet, but that the mallet-headed chisel is a very ancient and enduring design.

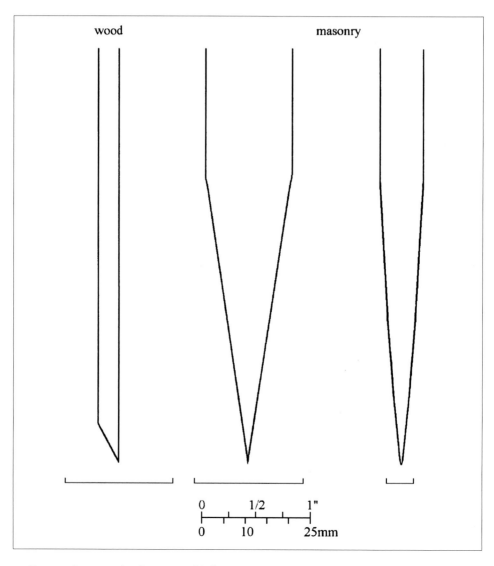

21 Cross-sections, wood and masonry chisels

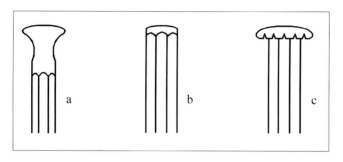

Left: 22 Mallet-head, hammer-head, and well-used hammer head

Opposite left: 23 Roman mallet-headed chisel. *After Manning 1984*

Opposite right: 24 Punch and pitcher

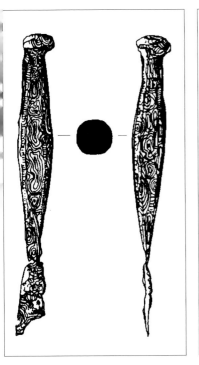
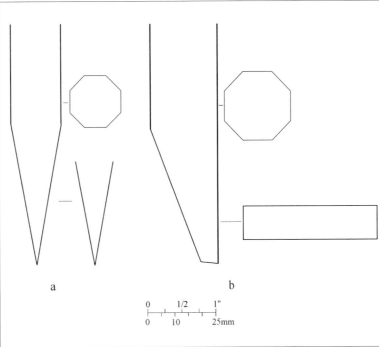

a   b

```
0      1/2      1"
0      10      25mm
```

The punch is a chisel-like tool drawn out to either a point or a narrow cutting edge (2-3mm, ⅛in) and struck with a hammer (*19d* and *24a*). It is made from similar stock to the chisel, with the thickness dependent on the heaviness of the work. As with chisels, the body of a punch may be much thinner for fine use by a carver. A point is a similar tool, but is either much lighter and finer, or struck with a mallet for use on softer stones. The extent to which the point of a punch is drawn out will tend to be greater for use on soft stone than for heavy work on hard stone.

The claw is in effect an ordinary chisel with deep nicks in the blade, and is used for roughing out the stone after the use of the punch. The teeth vary widely in size and form, depending on the initial design and the degree of wear, and may be pointed or have short cutting edges.

The gouge is curved in end view, exactly as a woodworking gouge, and was certainly known to the Romans (*25*) as well as to the modern mason (*19j*).

The bullnose chisel has a cutting edge curved in elevation but flat in end elevation (*19i*) and a possible Roman example is shown in *26*. Both the gouge and the bullnose are used for working concave surfaces, with the bullnose preferred for circular-circular-sunk work, as in the interior of a stone bowl.

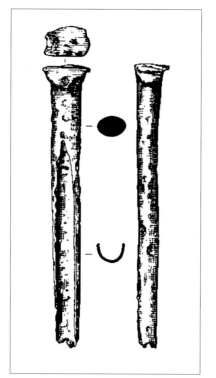

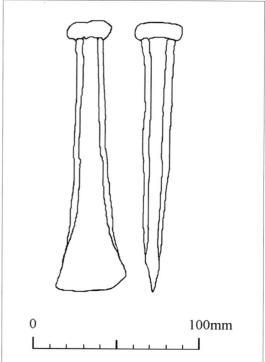

Above left: 25 Roman gouge. *After Manning*

Above right: 26 Roman bullnose chisel from Germany. *After Röder*

Right: 27 The nicker, used for splitting smaller stones

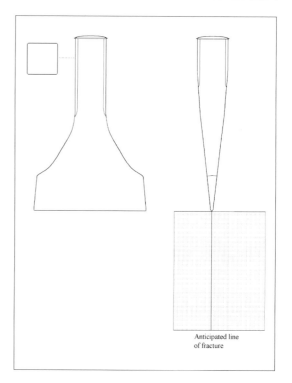

0   100mm

Anticipated line
of fracture

The pitcher, or pitching tool, shown in *figure 24b*, has not been found in ancient contexts but the use of this tool, or something similar, has provisionally been identified by the author at Birdoswald. Its principal features are a thick shaft of at least 25mm (1in) across, and a blade which is about 5mm (0.25in) thick at the cutting edge where there is a slight bevel. It is used for removing large pieces of stone with a single blow of a mason's hammer, ideally applied at right angles to a reasonably flat face.

The nicker (*27*) somewhat resembles the bricklayers' bolster, but has a much shorter and thicker blade, the better to direct the hammer blow through the stone. Its use will enable stone up to perhaps 9-10in (225-250mm) bed height to be split with remarkably clean faces; they may be slightly concave or convex, but in general will be roughly square to the beds and joints. This tool has not been identified in Roman contexts, but rusted remains would not look obviously different from a 3in chisel.

WORKING STONE

The detailed dressing, or working, of stone for the Wall is one of the more complex aspects of the building. There are two different types of skill involved, each requiring a different approach and learning time, exemplified by the different types of masonry visible on the Wall.

Squared rubble

Production of squared-rubble facing stones will have been something which most legionaries experienced as a normal part of their service. Julius Apollinaris, soon after joining his legion, gave thanks to Serapis that owing to his rapid promotion as a *librarius* (clerk) he was able to stand around all day while others were cutting stone (*P. Mich* VIII, 466). This suggests that it was a task which might be given to a newly joined legionary. It is in fact not a difficult skill to acquire, although there will be different degrees of achievement. The legions carried skilled stonemasons on their books (*Digest* 50, 6, 7, quoting Tarruntenus Paternus (late second century)), and these in more normal times would either have carried out the more accurate working themselves or would have been able to exercise greater supervision.

Examination of facing stones from the Wall shows that in many cases the beds and joints are either natural or result from splitting; any working is usually confined to a small amount of work with a punch to remove awkward projections. The dressing of a walling stone would all be done by eye, the judgement of the legionary being a sufficient standard to produce stones of approximately the right dimensions.

The faces are sometimes split but often roughly worked to give an unevenly rounded face. The tools used were principally the axe, the punch, and the (walling) hammer, and the stone was largely cut by their direct action. The use and effect of these tools has been fully described elsewhere (Hill 1981; Hill and David 1995) and will not be repeated here.

When reducing the surface with a punch used in the normal way, a series of roughly parallel furrows will be produced. Crossing these at right angles is a quick way of reducing peaks, but these will tend to disappear without leaving a second series of furrows; the diamond broaching[1] seen on the Wall is a deliberate finish. The intermittent occurrence of these stones is most likely to result from the whim of a legionary or his centurion rather than for consistent decorative effect.

The product of the work so far described is a stone which is usually approximately rectangular on elevation, with a flattish or roughly rounded face, and with beds and joints which are tapered to allow the stone to fit with its neighbours without great accuracy in dressing. The degree of exactitude required is not great. It is best if the beds are very roughly flat but with tapered joints it is quicker to take off too much rather than too little. Given a few tools of the right quality, a little practice, and some muscle development, squared rubble may be readily produced by almost anyone, with little training.

Robert Rawlinson, quoted by Bruce (1851, 79), dealt with railway masonry by using uneducated labourers under educated foremen. This course was followed because of 'difficulty in dealing with the regularly educated mason' and the passage implies that this was because of the low degree of skill required in work 'not unlike the Roman Wall in character.'

As part of an exercise with a group of people with no experience of working stone, the present author split a large natural slab into lengths. After only a few minutes, the group was immediately producing walling stones approximately 230 x 305 x 230mm (9 x 12 x 9in) in between four and six minutes *each*. The work was carried out using a 2.5lb (1.13kg) hammer and a nicker to split the lengths into suitable sizes, and the individual stones tidied up using a pitching tool and a punch or axe. Very little of the latter work was required except on those stones which had not split cleanly. The slabs available for this work were of convenient size, and the operation on the single day the author was present perhaps went more smoothly than the norm, but the experience does point up the relatively simple nature of the work.

Gate piers and voussoirs

The working of the gate pier stones is a quite different matter from squared rubble. The piers are there to support and transmit to the ground the mass of the arch and the superimposed walling of the towers. Ideally they will be large stones with flat beds and, for practical purposes, this is what is actually achieved in every known case; the lowest achievement is at MC48, where some of the beds are distinctly uneven.

The voussoirs have similar characteristics, as can still be seen at MC37 and Birdoswald fort. Both voussoirs and pier stones called for dimension stone.

The quarried blocks would, of course, be larger than the finished size; the amount of excess stone would depend on the skill of the quarrymen and the nature of the quarry, but is unlikely to be less than 50-75mm (2-3in) all round. The first operation would be to work one bed straight in all directions to an acceptable degree; this seems to have been around 2-3mm in 300mm (up to 1/8in in 1ft). The tools used were principally the punch or pick, first in furrows and then in smaller and smaller pecks; reasonably enough, the occurrence of 'holes' up to 5-10mm deep was not seen as a problem. A blade, which might be an axe, an adze, or a broad chisel, might be used to clean the edges and, occasionally, areas in the centre of the bed; at various sites the marks of blades of 40-50mm (1.5-2in) have been identified.

From this bed, one of the faces would be worked, beginning with a marginal draft down each edge and squared off from the finished surface. Squaring from these drafts in turn would make the bottom bed parallel to the top at whatever bed height the stone would make – or to a predetermined height if needed. The drafts referred to were not always fully worked, and squaring from the face to the second bed would have been impossible. It is possible that the height was measured; it is noticeable that not all pier stones have their top and bottom beds exactly parallel, which would be consistent with measuring rather than squaring.

Drafts might be worked along the top and bottom of the faces, but sometimes the arris was marked by merely pitching off along a line to indicate the wall line. The faces were sometimes worked more or less flat, and sometimes left as rock faces. MC37 has mostly shallow rock faces dressed with a punch or pick in deliberate furrows, while the best surviving stone of the north gate of MC10 was worked with a good deal of care to give a reasonably straight face. The standards of work were remarkably varied, from good to very poor; this is discussed further below, in chapter 10.

The working of the stone to the required shape could have been carried out either at the quarry or at the building site, but in order to avoid transporting excessive weight, working at the quarry would be preferred wherever possible. Squared rubble could not be damaged even when carelessly transported, and the work to reduce excess weight would most sensibly have been carried out at the quarry. It is very likely that the quoins needed for the turrets and towers will have been modified on site from stone worked at the quarry. In practice, the amount of work will have been small as it is very rare for the quoins to be other than very rough returns, with the difference between quoin stones and ordinary walling stones so slight that it would hardly be worth separating the different loads. Carefully worked stone is very easily damaged, but even the gate piers are not particularly susceptible to damage owing to the generally rough nature of the dressing.

There is little doubt that all the stone for the Wall was worked at the quarry, with only final finishing of the gate piers carried out at, or close to, the point of building. While there is no direct evidence for this, there is an absence of the large quantities of masons' chippings which would have resulted from work on site. Signs of stone dressing adjacent to a building must be treated with caution; a very small amount of dressing produces an inordinately large quantity of chippings, which of course take up a greater volume than the solid stone; the increase is around 40 per cent. A simple example will illustrate the point.

A stone in the base of the north-east pier of the south gate of MC42 is now approximately 585 x 900 x 450mm (23 x 35.5 x 17.7in), with faces C and D 230 and 400mm (9in and 15.75in) long respectively (28).

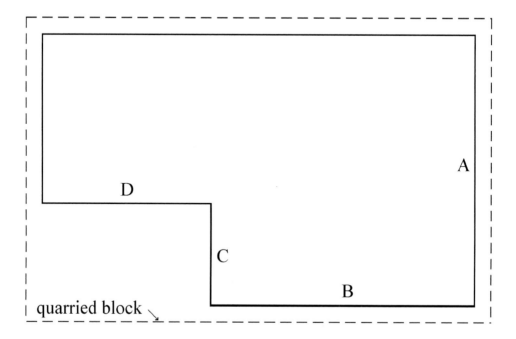

28 Waste in working a pier stone

If it were delivered from the quarry as a rough block no more than 50mm (2in) bigger all round than the final size, reduction to the required dimensions, with the internal return, would produce 4m² (45 sq.ft) of chippings 50mm (2in) thick. Each gateway contained some 36-40 stones in the piers and, allowing that half of them would not have internal returns, the chippings would cover 150m² at 50mm thick (1600 sq.ft at 2in thick). There has been no find of chippings amounting to anything like this figure. It is worth noting that the saving in weight by working the example at the quarry rather than on site is around 408kg (900lb).

Inscriptions

One aspect of working stone which was occasionally required was the cutting of the dedicatory inscription. First, the slab has to be prepared. Dressing of the slab involves very much the same techniques as for other worked stone. If the centre was to be a sunken panel, only sufficient of the face would be worked to allow for the width of the surround. To form a sinking like this not only takes longer than a simple flat surface, but takes a rather higher degree of skill and care if anything like a plane surface is to be achieved. Similarly, mouldings around this sinking are more difficult to execute than mouldings which run the full width of the stone to show their profile at both ends. The need for this level of skill is noticeably absent on milecastle inscriptions which are plain slabs.

Letter-cutting is almost invariably carried out with the stone in a near vertical position, allowing dust and chips to fall clear rather than lying to fill the letters and obscure the work.

The V-cut letter is cut-in from each side, working up each side of the letter. The chisel cuts forwards (upwards) along the length of the letter rather than cutting into the stone parallel to the axis of the letter. The chisel is normally used with a small hammer.

Finishing of the letters will involve cleaning the profile with the chisel in small, light cuts; the cut surfaces of very large letters may be rubbed with an abrasive stone, such as a carefully worn slip of sandstone. Lightly abrading the surface of the inscription with a larger slip of stone will clean the edges of the letters to some extent.

The above refers to the cutting of high-quality inscriptions with letters properly formed according to the style or fashion intended. On the Wall, the better inscriptions are normally found in the forts. *RIB* 1427 from Halton, commemorating the work of legion VI, is an excellent example of the craft of the letter-cutter and must have been the work of a properly trained man. The inscription from the east gate of Greatchesters (*RIB* 1736), on the other hand, has execrable lettering and layout; the unit responsible is not named. *RIB* 801, found near the east gate of Moresby on the Cumberland Coast, commemorates the work of legion XX on a slab which carries stylised foliage decoration rather than mouldings; like the Greatchesters inscription it is dated to post-AD 128 and is of similar surface area. It is not easy to determine which of the three inscriptions represents the norm – there are so few Hadrianic inscriptions of any quality surviving from the Wall that study is difficult. The three quoted are the only Hadrianic fort dedication inscriptions to survive.

The milecastle inscriptions, though less good than those from the forts, generally show some desire to produce a work of dignity, even if the best-trained legionary letter-cutters were busy elsewhere. However, they tend to have a distinctly amateur appearance (e.g. *RIB* 1638 from MC38, and *RIB* 1852 from MC47) when compared to the better fort inscriptions but the very attempt at quality introduces idiosyncratic styles which allow some identification of the hand at work.

The cutting of the centurial stones on the curtain wall seems generally to have been left to whoever was nearest to the centurion when the stone was called for; the almost uniformly poor quality of these records suggests that the occasional ansate panel was the whim of a bored legionary or his enthusiastic centurion rather than a serious attempt to produce work of any quality (e.g. *RIB* 1387, 1408). They were passing records rather than permanent statements for display. The tool commonly used for their cutting is the punch.

Large inscriptions are invariably on slabs which are thin in proportion to their visible area, simply to save weight; they are typically 100-150mm (4-6in) thick. *RIB* 1736 from Greatchesters is 1120 x 810 x 110mm (44 x 32 x 4.3in) and weighs in the order of 230kg (508lb); it could just about have been set in place by four men.

SETTING–OUT AND TEMPLETS

In the sense used in this section, setting-out is the process of making full size drawings of masonry details; 'details' means anything other than plain walling. The cross-sections of mouldings are drawn out, as well as elevations of features which are too large to be contained in a single stone. A monolithic arched window head could have been scribed directly onto the stone, a milecastle arch could not. In the medieval period there is ample evidence for setting-out, usually done on a prepared plaster floor.

There is limited but good evidence for setting-out drawings in the Roman period. Haselberger (1985 and 1995) has shown that the portico of the Pantheon was set-out on the paving alongside the mausoleum of Augustus, and that four centuries earlier the Greek builders of the temple of Apollo used the floor and lower walls of the temple for setting-out the upper parts. The worked stones were not checked directly against the drawings. Not only is the picture of masons attempting to move their large stones onto the drawing an impractical one, but in the case of the temple of Apollo some of the drawings were on vertical surfaces making such a practice impossible. At this temple most features were set-out as half-elevations, as with medieval and modern practice.

The purpose of these often very complex drawings was to establish stone sizes and to make the templets[2] from which the mason worked; there is in fact no other way in which they can be used. The drawing of the pediment of the Pantheon included the ashlar beneath the cornice, the only purpose of which must have been to give the sizes for the ashlar. This apparently simple point actually shows a high degree of sophistication.

No such drawings have been found on the Wall, although elevations of the gate arches will have been essential to give the face moulds for the voussoirs. These are probably the only elements which needed any serious setting-out; the very roughly worked chamfered string course was a simple affair which will have been worked to given dimensions. Elements of the internal buildings of forts, especially the entasis of the large columns, will have needed more in the way of setting-out. It is by no means impossible that standard templets were kept in the legionary drawing offices, and it would certainly have been an eminently sensible practice.

The use of templets, to transfer the form of moulding sections and face and bed moulds from full size setting-out drawings to the stone, is well-documented from medieval times onwards (Salzman 1952). The material was generally wood. The author has so far been unable to find any direct evidence for their use in Roman times; the fact that in the Wall area it is very rare for the two ends of a moulding to have the same profile indicates that their use was not universal. However, the existence of setting-out drawings shows that, at times, templets were used.

Templets would have been unnecessary for the gate piers as the stones have a simple plan. Small sketches on writing tablets, with dimensions, to give the plan and the elevation, would have been sufficient. It would not even be necessary to determine the length of the stones in elevation in advance. All the supervising officer had to do was to note the length of the stone used for the first course and make sure that the next course was longer or shorter. These sketches need not have been to scale, although the Greeks, and presumably the Romans, did understand the use of scale drawings. An example of what was needed is shown in *figure 29*. The upper sketch gives the dimensions of the plan, and the lower two are completed as stones are worked.

Working in this way would accommodate changes in bed heights in the

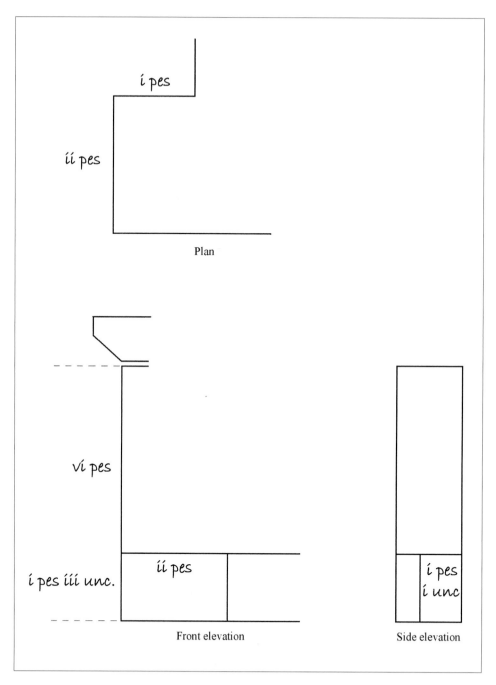

i pes

ii pes

Plan

vi pes

i pes iii unc.

ii pes

Front elevation

i pes i unc

Side elevation

Above: 29 Production and quantities sketch for a gate pier

Opposite above: 30 Cross-section of quarry, showing stone beds and bedding planes

Opposite below: 31 Ideal orientation of bedding planes in an arch

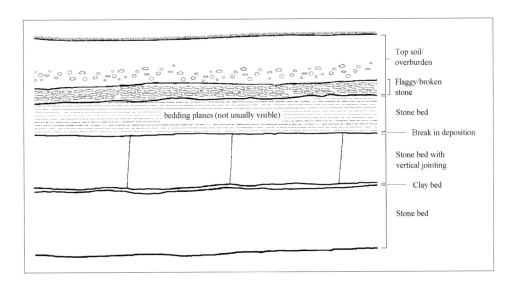

Top soil/
overburden

Flaggy/broken
stone

bedding planes (not usually visible)

Stone bed

Break in deposition

Stone bed with
vertical jointing

Clay bed

Stone bed

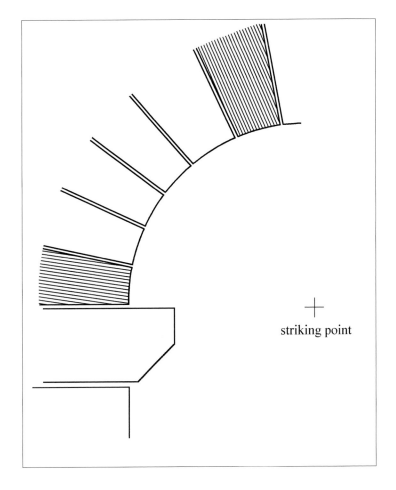

striking point

quarry without having to spend time and trouble to find beds which would produce stones to suit a predetermined list of dimensions. But however the work was organised it does not seem to have been universally successful. There are straight joints on the north-west pier of the south gate of MC42, and the ragged outer ends of the piers can hardly have been carefully planned.

ORIENTATION OF THE STONE

In an ideal world the bedding plane of the stone should be horizontal, as it lay in the quarry (30). The exception to this is voussoirs, where the bedding planes should lie on the radius of curvature at right angles to the line of thrust (31).

In practice it is not always possible to obtain a stone of sufficient bed height for something like an inscription or a column shaft, and these stones are often worked with the beds lying in a vertical plane parallel to the wall face (face bedded). The dedicatory inscription from Haltonchesters (RIB 1427) is a case in point, where the face bedding of the stone is shown by the way in which the surface has lifted.

WORKING STONE FROM ROMAN QUARRIES ALONG THE WALL

Samples of stone from several quarries were worked by the author to assess their suitability for pier stones and ease of working. In descending order they were:

Black Pasture (near Chesters fort)
Fallowfield Fell (near Chesters fort)
Queen's Crag (near Housesteads)
A stone from Harrow Scar, near Birdoswald (precise origin unknown)
Poltross Burn (close to MC48)

The first two were excellent stones, working easily and capable of taking a good finish; both stones were also suitable for lettering. Queen's Crag and the Harrow Scar stone were very good and would have been suitable for large dressed stones. Poltross Burn, a contact-metamorphosed sandstone, was the most intractable and not fit for producing good work. In addition, a common walling stone, surplus following excavation and consolidation near T39b, was obtained. It was coarse in texture and extremely hard; sparks were raised when chiselled. It would not have been suitable for pier stones without a considerable cost in labour and time.

4

LIME, SAND, AND MORTAR

In building the Wall, lime mortar was used for bedding the facing stones and for bonding some of the rubble of the core in those few areas where clay was not used.

LIME

Lime, as used in mortar, is obtained by heating limestone (calcium carbonate) in a kiln over several days to a temperature of between 900° and 1200°C which, with a loss of 50 per cent in weight, results in the formation of calcium oxide, or quicklime; the burning of a limestone containing a high proportion of magnesium carbonate will of course also give magnesium oxide. The addition of water to quicklime converts the oxides to hydroxides, known as slaked lime; when allowed to stand in an excess of water this yields a material known as lime putty.

Low firing temperatures are likely to lead to lumps of unburnt lime. Poor slaking leaves unslaked lumps which may later react with moisture in the building and can cause structural problems.

Cato describes the use of a flare kiln (*32*) in which a single charge of limestone is calcined by a fire beneath the charge, the lime extracted and the kiln recharged, over a period of four or five days This yields a whiter lime than that produced in a draw kiln, where alternate layers of limestone and fuel are loaded and the burning is continuous, with the lime drawn out from the base as it falls through a grid. The length of burn depends entirely on the heat produced by the fire.

Simpler kilns are also known from Roman Britain. These are clamp or sow kilns, in which alternate layers of stone and fuel were formed into a shallow pile and covered with turf before firing. The product of these kilns is uncertain in quality, but they remained in use until recent times.

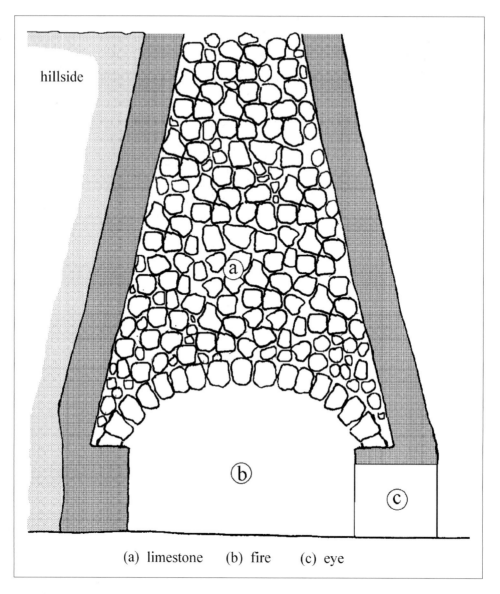

hillside

(a) limestone   (b) fire   (c) eye

32 A flare kiln for burning lime

There is only one certain Roman lime kiln known in the Wall area, alongside the Knag Burn close to Housesteads. Lime kilns are normally sited in, or close to, the limestone quarries to avoid transport of the raw stone.

There are two possible references to lime burning in the Wall area, pre-dating the Wall by some 20 years. One of the Vindolanda writing tablets refers to men being sent '... to the kilns'; these could be either lime or pottery/tile kilns

(Bowman and Thomas 1994, document 18). A second tablet is quite definite: 'to burn stone' (ibid., document 156).

Limestone which is pure calcium carbonate, or which contains inert impurities, yields *non-hydraulic* lime which sets by the absorption of carbon dioxide from the atmosphere, to produce a crystalline carbonate of lime. Setting may not begin for several months, and then only at the surface. In very thick walls full setting may well never take place in the interior, but this is often advantageous. Such lime can be kept for months so long as protected from the atmosphere, and indeed benefits from such maturing.

For ordinary building purposes it is not necessary to allow the slaked lime to mature to produce lime putty which is unlikely in the extreme to have been used in building the Wall. Instead, the method known as dry-slaking is used. Here, the lumps of quicklime are put in a ring of sand, sufficient water added to reduce the lumps to powder, and then mixed with the sand. Ideally, this material, known as 'coarse stuff,' is screened to remove lumps of unburnt lime and over-size aggregate. When mixed up again with more water it is ready for use after only a few hours. The dry-slaking method is ideal for the production of large quantities of mortar, and much quicker than using lime putty, which is more appropriate for plastering and stucco work. The method of slaking does not affect the speed of setting, which is entirely dependent on the chemical composition of the lime.

Solid ashlar walls rely on the massiveness of the construction and the careful bonding of the stones for stability, but rubble walls rely to some extent on the strength of the mortar and here a stronger lime is preferable.

Limestones which contain argillaceous (clayey) material yield feebly, moderately, or eminently *hydraulic* limes. Until modern production methods gave lime of exceptional purity, it was normal for limes to be impure and thus likely to be more or less moderately hydraulic. Where limestone occurs in association with clays, any clay put into the kiln with the stone will add to the hydraulic nature of the lime. Slaking is slower and less violent than non-hydraulic limes, taking from a few minutes upwards. Setting of hydraulic limes is by the combination of water with the silicates and aluminates of lime, formed at the time of burning, to form hydrated calcium silicate and hydrated calcium aluminate crystals. The eminently hydraulic limes, being little dependent on exposure to the atmosphere, will set under water. Analysis of mortar from the curtain wall at Sycamore Gap (near MC39) showed it to be an extremely durable and still effective hydraulic mortar, probably due to the use of the local highly siliceous Four Fathom limestone.

Any lime can be converted to a hydraulic lime by the addition of a material which has constituents which will combine with free lime to form an insoluble cementitious compound. Such a material is known as pozzolana, after Pouzzuoli from where the Romans obtained supplies of natural materials of volcanic origin. Similar natural materials are quite widely available. Artificial pozzolanas are made from, among other things, pounded brick and tile; such materials were commonly used by Roman builders (*opus signinum*) where strength and waterproofing were important. There is no record of their use in building the Wall.

The burning of lime requires the quarrying of limestone of a suitable kind, the collection and transport to the kiln of large quantities of wood (and perhaps coal which was available to the Romans in the Wall area) for use as fuel, and the transport of the finished product to the building site.

If the dry-slaking method were adopted, then it would probably be simplest to slake at the kiln and transport the coarse stuff to site. This would reduce the quantity of water to be taken to the site, and would mean that all sand would first go to the kiln site rather than to many individual sites.

If the coarse stuff were made at the site, then the quicklime could be carried in barrels on pack animals. The barrels would have to be tight and proofed against ingress of moisture; any inadvertent slaking while in transit could have a serious effect on the animals. Similarly, if the lime were wet-slaked, it could also be carried in barrels, or skins.

SAND

Lime is normally mixed with sand both to increase its bulk and to reduce cracking as the lime sets; sand also aids the setting of non-hydraulic limes. Sand, unless carefully washed, almost always contains clayey matter and silt, which can affect both the workability and subsequent analysis of the mortar. The cleanliness and relative uniformity of sand produced today relies on mechanical washing and grading, something not available to the Roman builder.

Sand will have been available both in large pits and down the slope from any outcrop of sandstone; Fallowfield Fell, for example, shows large pockets of sand at the surface in the small valley below the quarry face.

WATER

Water was required in large quantities, for slaking the lime, mixing the mortar, and wetting down the larger stones in dry weather. Each cubic metre of mortar takes about 370 litres of water to slake and mix (3 gallons for each cubic foot). Although there are abundant rivers and streams in the general area of the Wall, the builders could easily have found themselves up to half a mile away from the nearest water source, and on the crags this was over difficult terrain. The cleanliness of the water, in terms of detritus and vegetable matter, is unlikely to have been a matter of concern. Transporting the water was presumably by means of skins or barrels carried on mules or carts.

MORTAR MIXES

The proportion of sand to lime should be such that the lime fills the voids between the sand grains, usually 3:1 sand:lime. Vitruvius recommends a sand:lime mix of either 2:1 or 3:1. Analysis of mortar from Willowford Farm has suggested that the proportions by volume were roughly 1:1 sand:lime. Excavations of the Wall at Denton yielded bedding mortar in the proportions of about two parts of sand to one of lime.

It must be remembered that the mixing of mortar is neither an especially skilled job nor an exact science; measuring by volume, normally reckoned by the shovelful, can be very hit and miss. It depends on the conscientious application of the specification by the labourer and his ability to make his shovelfuls of consistent size. Furthermore, if the mix comes out too wet further material will be added to it, and the addition might be either lime or sand according either to the convenience or the judgement of the mixer. If the mix does not seem to work well, the fixer may ask for more lime to be added to the next batch. Sand, especially on a large work such as the Wall, might be delivered to one site from a number of small sources; this may well cause marked colour changes.

It will be clear that variations in mortar mixes cannot always be indicative of relative dating. Similarity of mortar can also be misleading. The hard white mortar generally regarded as typical of the Severan rebuild, also occurred in an Antonine context at Willowford Bridge. It is not usually possible, except on other evidence, to discriminate between original mortar and that of reconstruction.

5

SCAFFOLDING

Scaffolding is of two main types (*33*). The *putlog scaffold* has short poles (*putlogs*) resting on the wall at one end and supported by horizontal poles (*ledgers*) lashed to a row of uprights (*standards*) 1-2m from the wall.

The *independent* or *masons'* scaffold has an inner row of standards and there is no connection to the wall. Each pair of standards forms a bay of scaffolding, and each set of ledgers and putlogs form a *lift*.

For stability there may be *braces*, which are long poles running diagonally across the face of the scaffold, their purpose being to restrict lengthwise racking of the scaffold. There may be *cross braces*, poles set at an angle connecting the inner and outer standards to restrict lateral racking. *Rakers* are poles running at an angle, usually around 60°, from the scaffold to the ground to resist overturning. *Guard rails* lashed to the standards at a height of about 1m above the working platform prevent workmen falling, and *toe boards* prevent men and materials slipping off.

There is also the *trestle*, where boards are laid between two trestles, or across two blocks of stone, used for temporary, low access. The several types of scaffold may be combined in a single wall face.

It has been suggested that, given the width of the Wall, scaffolding would not be needed, but this is not practical. The alternatives would be men climbing the core at the ends of sections, or using ladders or scaffold towers against the built portion. Men and materials would then have to move along the core to reach the work site. But walking over the core, whether it were dry-laid, or clay or mortar bonded, would be immensely difficult. The rubble core would make for a difficult footing when carrying heavy loads and the stones would move, causing undue pressure on the newly laid facing stones.

Furthermore, without scaffolding those laying the facing stones would have had to stand on the core. As the core would need to have been built up to within one or two courses of the top, the fixers would have been bent nearly double, while constantly handling heavy stones, for the duration of the project. A few men would certainly have to stand on the core in order to tip rubble into the middle and to tip and spread clay or mortar, but the picture of the core as a highway for the provision of all materials and as a platform from which to fix the facing stones is simply not practical.

Certainly there is no alternative to the use of scaffolding for building the turrets where the side and south walls are only 900-1200mm (3-4ft) thick. This is similar to the thickness of the *horrea* walls at Birdoswald, where unequivocal evidence for scaffolding has been found. The fact that there is as yet no clear evidence available from the turrets for the use of scaffolding cannot be taken as evidence that it was not used, and the same must be true for the building of the curtain wall.

Scaffolding in Roman Britain

There is ample evidence for the Roman use of scaffolding, both in Britain and the empire (*34*). A few sites are reviewed here to illustrate the point.

At Birdoswald, there is very good evidence for the use of scaffolding in building the *horrea* (granaries). The standards used were in post holes 200mm (8in) diameter, but no indication was found as to the diameter of the posts. The four putlog holes (one pair in each of two bays), which went right through the wall, were between 140 and 165mm (5.5-6.5in) square, but there is no indication of the size of the putlogs.

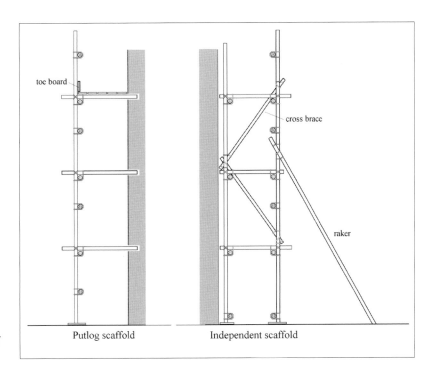

33 Types of scaffold

Putlog scaffold   Independent scaffold

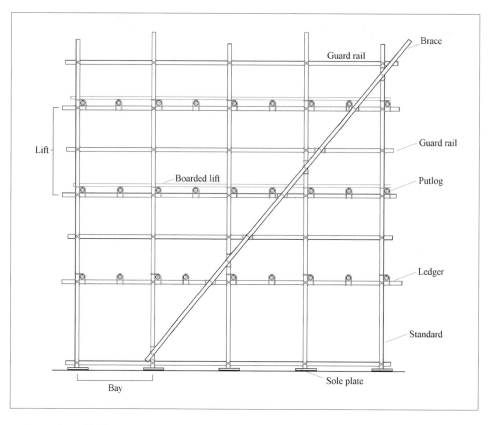

34 Parts of a scaffold

The standards were spaced at horizontal intervals of 1300mm (51in), and the putlogs at 1550 and 1700mm (61in and 67in). The offsets allow for the putlogs to lie on the outside of each pair of standards to give maximum support to the ends of the decking adjacent to the buttresses. The existence of the buttresses may have dictated the spacing of the standards, making it unsafe to use these figures on their own to establish normal Roman practice. It is clear, however, that a spacing of around 1600mm (63in) between the putlogs was considered safe. The first lift seems to have been at a height of 2m (6ft 6in), which would have allowed movement around the base of the scaffold.

The Jewry Wall at Leicester shows several rows of large putlog holes at horizontal intervals of 1500mm (5ft); the vertical interval is a little less. The standing wall of the *frigidarium* at Wroxeter ('The Old Work') shows putlog holes running through the thickness of the wall. They are in 1200-1500mm (4-5ft) vertical lifts, but there is not sufficient remaining to show the horizontal spacing of the putlogs.

35 Putlog hole at Ravenglass bathhouse

The bathhouse at Ravenglass gives good evidence for the use of a putlog scaffold, and is on a scale comparable to Hadrian's Wall; the height to the wall plate may have been 3.5m (11ft 6in). The spacing of the putlogs is at horizontal intervals of 1200-1500mm (48-60in). This is to some extent affected by buttresses, doors, and windows, but one wall may indicate what the 'normal' spacing would be. There is a putlog hole well to either side of a doorway, with an interval of 3000mm (10ft) between them; this is by any measure too long a run between putlogs and one in the position occupied by the door would be necessary. An intermediate inner standard against the wall, and between the door jambs, to carry the inner end of a putlog would reduce the interval to about 1500mm (5ft). This does suggest that this might be the normal spacing, as seen at the Jewry Wall. The vertical spacing ranges from 1140-1370mm (45-54in), averaging 1270mm (50in).

Impressions in the mortar inside the putlog holes give clear evidence of the size and form of putlogs used. The majority were round poles 100mm (4in) diameter, with occasional use of split poles to give half-round putlogs up to 150mm (6in) wide by up to 110mm (4.5in) deep (35). The putlog holes go through the walls, but both mortar impressions and the position of core stones indicate that the putlogs themselves were not always continuous poles but went rather less than half way through the wall.

The best contemporary illustration of scaffolding is from the tomb of Trebius Justus. This shows a single lift of independent scaffold; it is of no relevance for judging dimensions, but shows a guard rail at one end and a cross brace at the other.

THE EVIDENCE FOR SCAFFOLDING ALONG THE WALL

The evidence for scaffolding on the curtain wall is non-existent. Considerable parts of the Wall have been dismantled prior to rebuilding, and no clear evidence of putlog holes has been found. However, it is not necessary to use a putlog scaffold at all: the Wall could have been built using an independent scaffold, with an inner line of standards.

Settings for the feet of the standards have not been found in excavations along the line of the Wall, but it is not in fact essential for the feet of the standards to be sunk into the ground as they may be stood on a sole plate of a thick board or a stone slab, and thus little or no sign would be left. The rocky nature of the ground along the central sector, where the most extensive excavations of the curtain wall have taken place, also limits the likelihood of traces of the uprights being found.

THE PROBABLE NATURE OF THE SCAFFOLDING

Until the early twentieth century most scaffolds were still of wood, in the form of poles lashed together with rope. If sufficient young trees were not available, mature trees could be split to size. The trees typical of the area were oak, alder, birch, and hazel, with some elm and pine, all of which could have been useful in constructing scaffolds.

The figures for the size of scaffold poles which can be extrapolated from the Birdoswald and Ravenglass evidence accord reasonably well with early twentieth-century practice for masons' timber scaffolds. Standards at this time were typically 3-9m (10-30ft) long, 125mm (5in) diameter at the base (unless cut down from larger timber, scaffold poles were usually tapered), 1200-1500mm (4-5in) apart, and resting on sole plates; putlogs were 75mm (3in) square, spaced at no more than 900mm (3ft) apart. The Roman putlogs were slightly more substantial and their spacing slightly greater, as shown by the Birdoswald *horrea* and the Ravenglass bathhouse. Alder, poplar, fir, and ash were used for scaffold poles in medieval building with alder predominating for the uprights, lashed together with ropes of withies or bast (fibres from the flax plant).

It is not known what Roman builders used to board out the working lifts. Medieval practice was to use hurdles and it would be reasonable to assume the same for Roman builders.

The quantity of scaffolding required is difficult to estimate with any accuracy, as it is not possible to determine what the Roman army considered to be safe working practice. However, it is worth making an attempt, based on what is known of Roman scaffolding, on medieval and early twentieth-century practice, and on reasonable assumptions. In the absence of putlog holes on the Wall the design is for an independent scaffold.

The standards are taken as 5.5m (20ft) high on the north side, 4.6m (15ft) on the south, with an average diameter of 100mm, standing 1.22m (4ft) from the face of the wall, connected by ledgers at 1200m lifts, with 1500mm (5ft) putlogs secured to the ledgers at both ends. There are three lifts each of four feet on the south side, which brings the top lift below the wall top but gives reasonable access for flagging of a wall walk, and four lifts on the north side to allow for building the parapet (36). The height of the standards allows for a guard rail on the top lifts, and there is an extra ledger connecting the feet of the outer standards.

The spacing of the standards is at 1500mm (5ft) centres, with a putlog at every standard. Even when not being used to support the decking, the full complement of putlogs and ledgers would be required to stiffen the scaffold. One diagonal brace might be expected for every two bays of the scaffold. The standards and putlogs might have been 125mm (5in) diameter at their thickest points, averaging 100mm, the ledgers similar, and the braces and guard rail perhaps 75mm diameter.

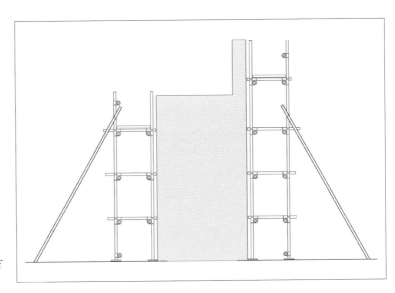

36 Section through the Wall showing design of proposed scaffold

The full length of the ledgers, braces, and guard rail would have been made up by overlapping and lashing. An extra 600mm has been allowed for this at each joint, with the assumption that poles were obtainable in no more than 5.5m (20ft) lengths.

The working platform would probably have been hurdles, with one lift fully decked out. The length of the hurdles would match the spacing of the putlogs, with either an extra putlog to support the end of touching hurdles, or the hurdles might be overlapped at the junctions. In the assessment of material, overlapping is assumed, with one 1800mm (6ft) hurdle to each 1500mm (5ft) bay.

Such a scaffold cannot be tied-in to the Wall, and must be prevented from overturning. This would best be achieved by 100mm x 6m (4in x 20ft) rakers running from the top of the third lift to the ground at 2.5-3m (8-10ft) from the foot of the scaffold; one raker to every three bays might be expected.

Building in squared rubble is a relatively rough process calling for speed rather than precision in the placing of the stones, and it would therefore be sensible to erect as long a run of scaffolding as possible to avoid frequent halts while the scaffolding was moved. What this length might have been is a matter of guesswork, and the following table uses a module of 30m (100ft), divided into 20 bays, which can be multiplied up as preferred. Scaffolding would be needed on both sides of the Wall at the same time.

For the module of scaffolding described the scaffold poles weigh about 8.5 tonnes, with another 1.5 tonnes for the hurdles. Each module (both sides of the Wall) would also have called for some 1360m (4460ft) of rope or withies for lashing the spars. The length of rope needed is based on 10ft per joint and must be seen as an absolute minimum.

Type	No. x length x dia.	Overlap	75mm poles	100mm poles
Standards (N)	42 x 6m x 100mm			252m
Standards (S)	42 x 4.6m x 100mm			193m
Ledgers (N)	9 x 30m x 100mm	22m		292m
Ledgers (S)	7 x 30m x 100mm	17m		247m
Putlogs (N)	84 x 1.5m x 100mm			126m

Putlogs (S)	63 x 1.5 x 100mm			95
Braces (N)	10 x 6m x 75mm		60m	
Braces (S)	10 x 6m x 75mm		60m	
Guard rail (N)	1 x 30m x 75mm	2.5m	33m	
Guard rail (S)	1 x 30m x 75mm	2.5m	33m	
Rakers (N)	10 x 6m x 100mm			60m
Rakers (S)	10 x 6m x 100mm			60m
Totals			186m (610ft)	1325m (4347ft)

Table 1 Scaffolding quantities for Hadrian's Wall: 30m module

The turrets and milecastle gate towers probably reached 10.7m (35ft) to the eaves, and needed more scaffolding in proportion to the curtain wall, in order to negotiate the corners and to allow an access hole in the interior scaffold (*37* and *38*).

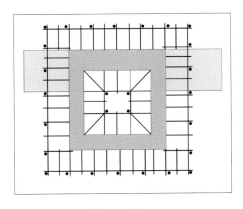

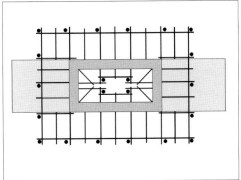

Above left: 37 Scaffolding for a turret

Above right: 38 Scaffolding for a milecastle tower

Using putlog scaffolds, a reasonable estimate of the scaffolding needed to take a turret to full height, in advance of building the adjacent curtain wall, is 1340m (4460ft) of poles, and 60m (200ft) of 1200mm (4ft) wide hurdles, the whole weighing just under 7 tonnes.

Again using a putlog scaffold, each tower on a type I or type II milecastle gateway would take 675m (2220ft) of poles and 30m (100ft) of hurdles for the exterior. The interior scaffold is difficult owing to the need to provide internal access for materials; using the scheme illustrated in *figure 36*, 200m (664ft) of poles, 4.2m (14ft) of 915mm (3ft) hurdles and 2400mm (8ft) of 600mm (2ft) hurdles would be required.

There would have been many gangs working at the same time along the length of the Wall, making heavy demands on the timber resources of a countryside which had to a considerable extent been cleared for agriculture (see chapter 1).

If each of the three legions had at any one time, say, five gangs taking curtain wall to full height, four gangs building milecastle towers, and two gangs completing turrets, the total requirement for scaffolding would have been about 45,720m (150,000ft) of straight poles to supply each legion. The provision of these large quantities of scaffolding may have been the major bottle-neck in the building programme.

6

HOISTING

TYPES OF LIFTING TACKLE

Raising a heavy weight vertically above a fixed point was not particularly difficult for Roman builders. They had ropes and the multiple pulley block, the windlass and the tread-wheel, and given the manpower the task was relatively simple. For loading a single item onto a cart a simple tripod, with pulley blocks at the head, would do, the cart being backed beneath the raised load. For heavy loads a sheer-legs might be used, as described by Vitruvius and shown on a bas-relief carving on the family tomb of the Haterii, dating from around AD 100. Power could be delivered either by a windlass set across the lower part of the legs, or by a tread-wheel on an extension of the axle (*39*).

This crane is, however, limited to moving the load forwards and backwards as there are no literary or sculptural references to the legs being mounted on a turntable. It may have been used to raise loads to the top of the building, where simpler tackle could take over for movement to the actual site of operations.

A single-pole derrick, which could easily be repositioned as required, is also described by Vitruvius (X, 2, 8-10). The pole has its heel set into the ground and held in place by stays on four sides. At the top of the pole a block with either single or multiple pulleys allowed weights to be hoisted with relative ease, but swinging them sideways would be a different matter. A simple derrick with a single block is shown in *figure 40*.

One problem with the derrick is that in order to swing the load sideways the supporting guys have to be eased and used as manoeuvring lines, an operation of potential danger. Like the sheer-legs, the derrick is best suited for simple movements up and down or backwards and forwards. Despite its drawbacks, the single-pole derrick has the great merit of simplicity, cheapness, and easy repositioning.

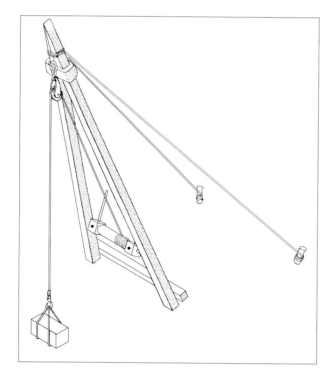

Left: 39 Sheerlegs

Below: 40 Pole derrick

Opposite: 41 Mast derrick

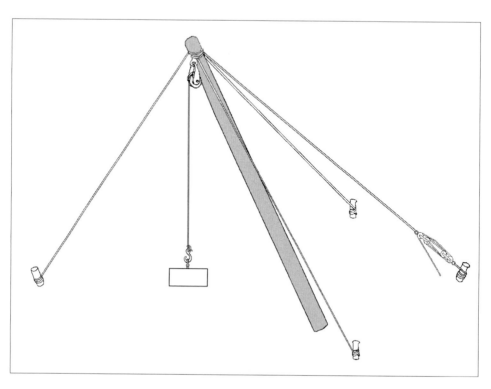

Vitruvius also mentions an 'upright' type, for which there have been several explanations. An upright post with a moveable jib might be what he means. This type of derrick consists of a jib whose heel is pivoted on the base of a fixed upright pole (*41*). The mast is supported by fixed guys; the height of the jib is controlled by a rope running from the head of the jib through blocks on the upright, and its inclination to right or left by separate guide ropes. The lifting tackle is independent of the support and control guys. This type of crane would have been suitable for building the piers and arches of the milecastle and fort gateways.

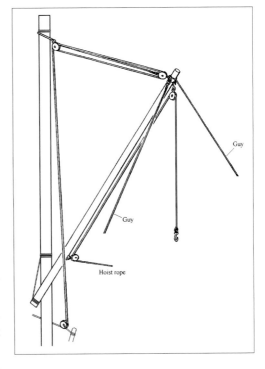

The use of lifting tackle in the quarry would probably be limited to loading the pier stones and voussoirs on to wagons for transport to the site. There may have been some need for moving large blocks away from the quarry face before they were cut down to manageable size. This does not, however, necessarily depend on having a crane close at hand. Various types of crane have in recent times been used for simply dragging stones from the quarry face to a point where they could be lifted. Equally, a block and tackle secured to a holdfast some distance from the face could have been used for dragging the stone along the ground.

The use of rollers for moving stone in the quarry must be considered. The major problem with their use is that both the ground surface and the underside of the block must be reasonably smooth unless the rollers are to be of inconveniently large diameter.

ROPES

Apart from the timber and iron needed for the construction of the crane, a supply of reliable ropes was necessary. The fall of a large block of stone from inefficient tackle is startling in its speed and almost instantaneous contact with the ground – or the quarryman. It takes about one fifth of a second for a stone to fall 2m.

O'Connor discusses the likely strength of ropes in Egyptian and Roman times, and concludes that 'It is possible, therefore, that the capacities of ancient ropes may not have been greatly different from modern [natural fibre] ropes.' It is probable, then, that little difficulty would have been experienced in providing rope to lift the modest weights encountered in building the Wall. The materials used were flax, grass and, in the east, papyrus and camel hair.

THE CAPACITY AND USE OF LIFTING TACKLE IN BUILDING THE WALL

The stones used in the curtain wall, averaging around 29kg (64lb) could easily have been moved by hand by one or two men. The very large stones used in the base of the Wall in some places (e.g. Great Hill and Heddon), weighing up to a quarter of a ton, could have been manhandled into place by rolling and levering without taking any harm. Loading onto a cart, if this were necessary, could be achieved by rolling up a plank.

In the initial scheme the only need for lifting tackle was in the building of the gateways of the 49 stone milecastles: 98 portals. After the fort decision was taken, there were a further 28 double- and 9 single-portal gateways, a total of 159 portals with 318 arches.[1]

The best-preserved milecastle gateway is the north gate of MC37. The average weight of the pier stones is around 510kg (1120lb), all much too heavy to be lifted without tackle. The same is true of the voussoirs, with an average weight of 283kg (624lb). It would have been possible to use hand-lifting for the stones of the north gate of MC39, which are significantly smaller than those at other milecastles.

One of the heaviest stones so far identified on the Wall is from the north gate at Chesters fort. The stone which formed jointly the foundation and first course of the north-east pier of the north gate is 860 x 1130 x 480mm (34 x 45 x 19in). Allowing 50mm all round for the quarried block, the weight will have been around 1.6 tons; lifting tackle will have been required to move this at all stages of production and building.

For building the Wall there was no need for cranes of the capacity and complexity of the Haterii sheer-legs, but there is one stone which called for a crane of twice that capacity. On the counterscarp of the ditch at Limestone Corner is a large block of basalt which has split into three pieces since it was deposited there. The overall measurements of the original block are 3000 x 1040 x 1400mm (10 x 3ft 5in x 4ft 7in). Basalt weighs 2950kg/m^2 (185lb per cubic foot), and the stone would originally have weighed just over 13 tonnes. A sheer-legs would be the most appropriate form of crane. There is no sign of the attachment of any form of tackle and it must have been lifted using rope slings.

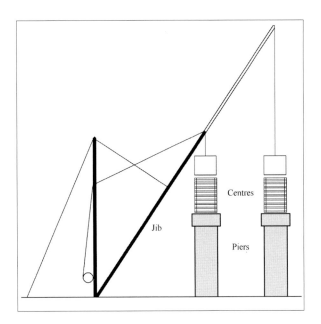

42 Using a mast derrick to build a milecastle gateway

The building of the gateways is dealt with in chapter 8, but it will be convenient here to look at the type and use of lifting tackle. *Figure 42* shows the use of a mast derrick.

The extrados of the arches stood about 4270mm (14ft) above ground level. If the derrick were to work at a minimum angle of 60°, and allowing 600mm (2ft) clearance for the topmost voussoir and another 600mm for the attachments and pulley blocks, the working height of the jib would be a minimum of 5.5m (18ft) at the arch nearest to the derrick. This gives a minimum length for the jib of 6300mm (20ft 10in) with the foot based 3.2m (10ft 5in) from the centre line of the arch.

If the derrick were to be based inside the milecastle for building all of a gateway (at some milecastles there is hardly room to base a derrick to the north) and for it to operate at the same minimum angle, the jib would have to be 11m (37ft 9in) long. The operating height of this jib would be almost 10m (33ft) from the ground.

The derrick could have been a smaller one and moved from inside to outside the milecastle, but the evidence from MC37 indicates that the southern piers of the north gate were incomplete when the northern ones were started, which suggests that building of both sides was proceeding in parallel. It would have been a generous provision of equipment if two derricks were used for each gateway.

Two post holes were found on the inner side of the *porta principalis sinistra* at Birdoswald. They are 3400mm (11ft) from the face of the tower; two or three times the width of a normal scaffold. The standards are 4500mm (14ft 6in) apart, about three times as wide as the normal spacing.

These post holes may represent provision for hoisting large stones. Weights of up to, say, 50kg (1cwt) are easily lifted using a simple jib projecting from the face of the scaffold; there is an overturning moment, but that is usually resisted by a well-built scaffold. For very heavy weights, a tower may be built onto the face of the scaffold, and the pull taken down within it.

Figure 43 shows a lifting jib with simple gin wheel; *figure 44* shows a tower which is consistent with the two posts joined by a slot at Birdoswald. The purpose of the slot would be to take a beam to restrain the horizontal movement of the windlass.

ATTACHMENT TO THE CRANE

A block of stone may be attached to the lifting tackle either by tying the main lifting rope around the block in a single rope hoist, by using a rope sling attached to the lifting hook, or one of the forms of mechanical attachment.

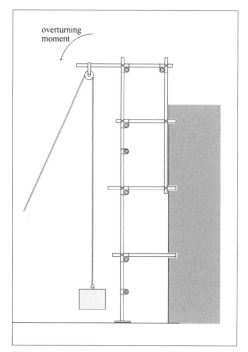
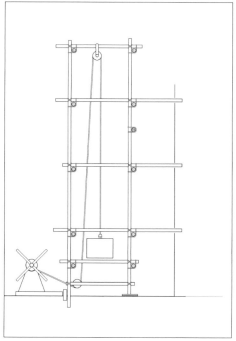

Above left: 43 Lifting jib

Above right: 44 Scaffold tower

Nippers and dogs

A convenient tool for lifting small blocks is the nippers, a scissor-shaped device, with the tips of the 'blades' turned inwards to form hooks (*45*). Working on a similar principle, but much more convenient to handle, are what are now generally known as 'chain dogs', 'rope dogs' or simply 'dogs'.

These have two separate hooks, each terminating in a ring, fitting into similar holes to those used for the nippers (*46*).

A rough, cone-shaped, shallow hole ('dog hole') is cut in each end of the stone, using a hammer and punch, an operation which takes a matter of seconds. A rope or chain is rove through the 'handle' end of the nippers or through the rings on the dogs, and slung from the lifting hook. When the strain is taken, the pull causes the hooks of nippers or dogs to bite into the holes and the stone to lift.

These holes are common on buildings and Roman bridges elsewhere in the empire but they are virtually absent in Britain. Only two examples of stones with dog holes are known to the author from Britain, both from Vindolanda; it may well be that there are more awaiting recognition.

Lewises

Nippers and dogs, especially the latter, are very suitable for quarry work as well as on buildings. Where large stones have to be butted tight up to their neighbours, and therefore cannot be gripped on the joints, some other device has to be used. Rope slings around the stone are simple but inconvenient as they are not easily removed when the stone is in place, and the usual method was the lewis. There are several types which are of some antiquity, the chain lewis (sometimes called the C-lewis after its shape), and the three-legged lewis.

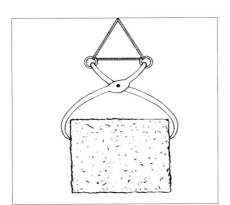

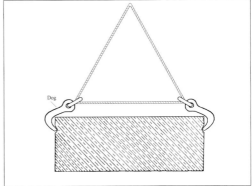

Above left: *45* Nippers

Above right: *46* Rope dogs

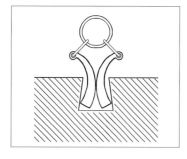 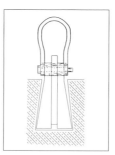 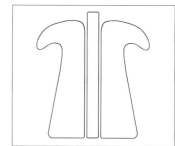

Above left: 47 Chain lewis

Above middle: 48 Three-legged lewis

Above right: 49 Roman three-legged lewis from Passau

The chain lewis consists of two curved pieces of iron, each one terminating in a ring (*47*). The two rings are connected by a third ring, forming a short chain which gives the name. The two legs are put back to back into a slot undercut at its short ends and when the strain is taken the lower ends of the legs are held against the undercut.

The three-legged lewis is still occasionally to be found in use today. The two outer legs are solid tapered bars (*48*), and thus less dependent on the strength of the metal than the chain lewis.

A Roman variant in Passau museum is very similar to the modern one, and the only difference is in the much simpler means of attachment to the hoist. Instead of a shackle and pin, the upper ends of the outer legs are curved downward, forming a hook to take a sling (*49*).

The lewis hole is rectangular in plan with the two long sides cut vertically; the short ends are undercut so that the length of the hole is greater at the bottom than the top. This is an important feature, and the only sure way in which a lewis hole can with certainty be distinguished from a hole cut for some other purpose. The angle of the ends when used with a modern three-legged lewis is something like 10°, or less, to the vertical. The grip must be at the bottom of the hole rather than the top, or the stone will break away. Owing to the difficulty of cutting a deep, narrow slot, a bent chisel is used (*19k*).

The width of surviving Roman lewis holes is mostly between 15 and 20mm. The lengths vary widely at Chesters, with the largest being over twice the length of the smallest. At Birdoswald, there is a consistency centred around 120-25mm long. Most, if not all, of the holes at both sites have clearly been reduced by working off the top bed of the stone after fixing, but this does not seriously affect the length, which will increase only slightly with the depth.

7

TRANSPORT

One of the biggest problems facing the Roman builders was transporting materials from quarry, kiln, and logging site to the building site.

MATERIAL	KG PER CUBIC METRE	LB PER CUBIC FOOT
Sandstone facing	2320	145
Basalt (whin)	2860	178
Clay	2000	125
Sand (coarse pit)	1611	100
Quicklime	960	60
Mortar	1600	100
Core stone	1760	110
Oak, green	1000	62

Table 2 Average weights of materials to be transported

Lime, sand, water, and clay would break down into loads of any convenient size. The facing stones weigh, on average, around 29kg (64lb) each, although in some parts the lower courses of the Wall incorporate much larger stones.

The pier stones for the milecastle gateways are between 129 and 739kg (285-1630lb). The merlon caps found on several sites had a transport weight of about 49kg/109lb, or 25kg/55lb for a half-cap. The milecastles and turrets needed beams, for upper floors and barrack roofs; the heaviest of these is likely to have been the turret-floor joists, estimated at around 81kg (180lb).

The fort gateways used on occasions very large stones. Chesters fort in particular has notably large stones in its gate piers, weighing between 1 and 1.4 tonnes. These weights assume that the stone was fully worked in the quarry. As the remains of lewis holes are often much too shallow to be serviceable it is certain that the top beds of some stones at Chesters were worked down after fixing and the transport weight will have been at least 10 per cent greater; that is between 1.1 and 1.5 tonnes. Several stones from the south and west gates at Housesteads are well in excess of half a tonne as now seen.

The tie beams spanning the *principia* basilica will almost certainly have been the largest timbers used in a fort. At Chesters, the span of the nave averages 8390mm (27ft 6in); giving an allowance for bearing of 300mm at each side, a beam of 9m (29ft 6in) will have been needed. Based on medieval practice, a beam 300mm (12ft) square might have been used, with a weight of 830kg/1830lb.

It is clear that the problems of transport would have been exacerbated in terms of individual load size, as well as simply of quantity, when forts were added to the line of the Wall. In most cases it would have been easy to reduce the dimensions of the larger stones; the fact that they were not so reduced indicates that their transport was not a serious problem.

METHODS OF TRANSPORT

Manual carrying
Where the material sources were very close to the Wall, animals would not have been necessary for the smaller items, and manpower would be substituted. This would be by means of buckets, baskets, or skins, on hurdles, or directly by the legionary, depending on the material.

For short carries, stones and turf could have been carried on the shoulders or backs of the soldiers, as shown on Trajan's column (e.g. scene lx). Weights of up to 50kg (112lb) could have been moved in this way over short distances. This limit would serve to move large core stones and most of the facing stones where the quarry was close to the line of the Wall.

The distances for manual carrying are not easy to determine. The British army in the early twentieth century saw wheeled (horse) transport as economical for distances of above 200yds and, by implication, the use of man-carrying for shorter distances.

The ideal device for moving materials over short distances, the wheelbarrow, does not appear to have been available to the Romans. Its origins seem to lie in first century AD China and the first record in the west is around AD 1200. Roman literature gives no word for a single-wheeled cart. But in Greece, in two inventories of a temple treasury and building equipment stores in Eleusis, there appears *monokyklos*, a single-wheeled cart, which can hardly be anything other than a wheelbarrow – unless it merely refers to a broken cart. However, as the language of the wheelbarrow owes virtually nothing to Latin, the use of the wheelbarrow must be discounted.

Pack transport

It is likely that where the distance from the source to the site was above that suitable for man-transport, carriage of items which would break down into manageable, balanced loads would have been by pack animal, of which each legion had at least several hundred. The historical use of pack animals for carrying building stone is well attested.

The mule was very widely used in the Roman world. The *Theodosian Code* (see below) refers to the use of mules for pulling the vehicles of the *cursus publicus*, and Trajan's Column shows army mules used for both traction and as pack animals. Josephus describes the Roman soldiers placing their baggage upon mules as they prepared to march (*Jewish War* III, v, 4). The use of the mule is not surprising, as he is more sure-footed, can work on a poorer diet, carry heavier loads, is less prone to sore back, and is generally hardier, than the horse.

Despite this, there is very little direct evidence for the use of the mule in Britain, or indeed in other provinces. Mules are not easy to identify from skeletal remains, and there has been very little study of equine dentition which seems to give the best means of differentiating between horse/pony and mule. A number of mules have very recently been identified at Vindolanda.

The mule is the result of a cross between a horse mare and an ass stallion. There is some evidence for asses (donkey is the English term for the domesticated ass) in Roman Britain, and if there were asses then there were probably mules. There seems no good reason to doubt that the mule was used by the Romans as extensively in Britain as in the rest of the empire.

It is also to be expected that the Romans used the local ponies found in Britain. Among the skeletal remains from Newstead were a number of ponies of between 11hh and 12.2hh which were probably used for baggage. Analysis of excavated equine remains at Corbridge from 1906-11 indicated that there must have existed in Roman Britain at least three types of horse: one around 14.2hh, and perhaps up to 15hh, which even today makes a respectable mount for a man; a type approaching the New Forest pony, of around 12.2hh; and one of the Exmoor type, around 11.2hh.

Loading of pack animals

Armitage and Chapman (1979) refer to the apparent abuse of mules in the Roman period, at least when employed in the service of the *cursus publicus*, and the considerable numbers of replacement animals which must have been available. Modern concerns for animal welfare should not be allowed to intrude on considerations of the likely loads placed on pack animals during the building of the Wall. There is ample evidence that in the nineteenth century military pack animals were often treated as disposable assets and at times very little consideration was given to their condition (Essin 2000, especially chapter 4).

There seems to be no direct evidence for the load of a Roman army mule or packhorse but as the size of the mule and pony seems to have changed little, later evidence ought to be relevant.

The modern Mk IV British Army pack saddle weighs 18kg (40lb) and a 14.2hh Highland pony is expected to carry this and a 160lb (73kg) payload for 15-20 miles a day. This type of animal is similar to those available to the Roman army. Some of the Defence Animal Centre training material allows a load of 310lb (140kg) for a mule.[1] Although the saddle is heavy in relation to the load, is it lighter than the one used in the early twentieth century. In fact it is quite possible to use a simple sawbuck pack saddle weighing as little as 3kg (7lb). This consists of two X-frames joined by short planks with well-padded panels beneath. Constable identifies a pack saddle on Trajan's Column (Cichorius No. 39) as being of this type.

In the eighteenth century packhorses were used to carry iron ore in Weardale; each animal carried two bags each of one hundredweight (102kg/224lb in total) in addition to the pack saddle. The horses used were Galloways, 12-13hh and apparently similar to the Dales pony. One must expect that they were well up to their loads, as no civilian contractor would risk rendering his animals unfit due to overwork. In the nineteenth century in the Yorkshire Dales the packhorse carried two pigs of lead, each weighing approximately 67kg (148lb), a pay load of 134kg (256lb).

The American army in the nineteenth century tended to prefer a mule of 13-14.2hh. Such a mule was expected to carry a payload of 91-114kg (200-250lb) on long marches. In the Second World War, Italian ponies and mules in the Apennines were loaded with up to 400lb (180kg), and sometimes more, for short hauls, and this in difficult country that was accessible only to the pack animal (Essin 2000). The Italian animals were 'smaller and lankier' than the American mule.

All the above indicates that the mule or pack pony could carry a payload of 91-113kg (200-250lb) on long marches. Difficult country reduces the load, but the topography of the Wall area in the central sector is undulating rather than rough. In building the Wall, the distances materials had to be moved were very short, and half the round trip would be unladen. In view of this, and the apparent abuse suffered by animals in the Roman world, it will here be accepted that the mules or ponies would carry a payload of at least 113kg (250lb), and probably considerably more.

Wheeled transport

Where conditions permitted, or where individual items were too heavy or would not break down into balanced loads, draught animals would have been used. Until the advent of the modern heavy horse, the ox has generally been preferred for very heavy loads or in poor conditions. Ox-drawn wagons are slower than those drawn by horse or mule, the former moving at about 2mph, the latter at 3-4mph.

Types and capacities of wheeled transport

There is no factual information available on the capacities of wheeled transport or the size and nature of teams used by the Roman army in the second century. The most detailed evidence for transport in the Roman world comes from the *Theodosian Code*. A decree of AD 357 issued by Constantius Augustus and Julian Caesar set limits of 1000 *librae* (VIII, 5, 8) for a *raeda*. A maximum weight on an *angaria* of 1,500 *librae* was given in AD 368 in a decree of Valentinian, Valens, and Gratian (VIII, 5, 30). In AD 385, Valentinian, Theodosius, and Arcadius set a limit of 600 *librae* on a *carrus* (VIII, 5, 47). The nature of these vehicles and modern equivalents of their capacities are given in the table.

TYPE	LIBRAE	KG	LB	
Angaria	1500	490	1080	4-wheeled wagon
Raeda	1000	328	722	4-wheeled wagon
Carrus	600	164	361	2-wheeled cart

Table 3 *Theodosian code*: capacity and type of vehicle

Mitchell argues that the Prices Edict of Diocletian implies that the *carrus* could have either two or four wheels, and that one type could carry a load of 1200 Roman pounds. This alone makes the use of the *Theodosian Code* for computing the number and type of carts or wagons needed for building the Wall an uncertain undertaking. One of the writing tablets from Vindolanda refers to the use of a *carrulum* (a diminutive of *carrus*) for carrying stone (Bowman and Thomas 1994, document 316). This confirms that carts or wagons were in use for transport of stone, but does not help with the capacity. By definition, a cart has two wheels and a wagon four.

The weight limits set by the *Code* are very low for substantial vehicles. It may be that the restrictions were aimed, in part, at reducing wastage of animals in unfamiliar hands when working on long-distance transport (the hire-car effect). The decree of Constantine Augustus notes that 'very many persons by means of knotty and very stout clubs force the public post animals … to use up whatever strength they have ….' The restrictions do not necessarily have any relevance to the usage of wagons by the army.

Despite their surprisingly low limits, the figures given in the *Code* have often been accepted, in part on the basis that ancient harness systems were very inefficient. Spruytte has shown that this was not necessarily so, and that two horses in breast collars of the ancient type could pull a load of 2150lb (975kg) gross, 970lb (440kg) nett, at the trot and on sand, which is one of the most unfavourable surfaces for traction. He also shows that 'a harness of this type, although less appropriate than the modern breast collar harness with traces, is in no way a hindrance to traction.'

Burford also rejects the notion that heavy transport could not be used in ancient times and that, while not necessarily routine, movement of heavy loads was not uncommon. She gives many examples of building stones weighing well in excess of the limits of the *Code*.

It is difficult to make use of representations of wheeled transport shown in sculpture. Carts of various types are shown on Trajan's Column and on sculptures but can provide no more than a generalised view.

However, scene cvii/285 on the Column shows a two-mule cart (*carrus*) piled high with what are believed to be tents (Lepper and Frere 1988, 261); it is not possible to see the number of tents, but an estimate of the weight carried may be made. Fragments of a tent from Vindolanda were reproduced in goatskin by the Ermine Street Guard. This tent, waterproofed with tallow, weighs 44kg dry and 51kg when wet (96lb and 113lb). Taking the capacity of a mule as argued above, the weight of two tents would be a reasonable, and even light, load for one pack mule. To make the use of a two-mule cart worthwhile, it must be assumed that it is carrying at least five wet tents and perhaps more, a weight of 257kg (565lb) at the least.

The modern type of shoulder collar for horses came in around the tenth century. But the yoke used for oxen has changed little and the technology of the medieval ox-cart was similar to that of the Roman period.

Salzman quotes figures for the carriage of lead from Caldstanes in Nitherdale to Boroughbridge in 1363, a distance of 20 leagues (about 60 miles) 'by high and stony hills and by miry roads'. The distance given is for the round trip. Two wagons, each drawn by 10 oxen, transported 24 fother (about 24 tons) of lead in 24 days.

If the average distance covered in a day was 15 miles, it would have taken four days to complete the round trip, and thus six such journeys could be made in the given time. Each wagon would therefore have carried 2 tonnes, four times the Theodosian limit. This is a large increase, but the facts are clearly stated and to reduce the increase even to three times the Theodosian level, that is one and a half tonnes, the oxen would have had to travel 20 miles a day and make eight journeys. While not impossible, this must be considered to be at the limit for working draught oxen. Oxen travel at '2-2.5mph and can work for seven or eight hours a day' and 'will travel 15 to 20 or even 24 miles a day under favourable conditions' (Veterinary Dept. 1908, 295, 300). But 'high and stony hills and miry roads' are not favourable and in that sort of country an ox-wagon would be lucky to average 2mph. 15 miles a day with a load of 2 tonnes is the more likely.

The limits in the *Code* are bureaucratic rules. The medieval capacity is an accountant's record of precisely what did happen, and apparently with animals and vehicles belonging to a private contractor. It may be assumed that the contractor would have been at least as careful of his animals as the Roman army would have been. If 10 oxen could pull a nett weight of 2 tons in the fourteenth century, it would be remarkable if they could not have managed something similar in the early second century; furthermore the loaded distances on the Wall will have been very short.

Cattle bones from Vindolanda are of the Celtic shorthorn breed, and some of the long bones are massive. This massivity may be due to inheritance from ancient stock such as the aurochs, or it may be the result of the Romans introducing large draught oxen (Seaward 1993, 110). Audoin-Rouzeau lists the withers height for cattle and shows an increase in the Roman period as compared to the Iron Age, with a small decrease especially around the eleventh to thirteenth centuries; by the fifteenth century the size was increasing again with the average being a little smaller than the Roman but with some animals reaching a greater size. It is clear that oxen available to the Roman army could have been larger than those in the fourteenth century, and were unlikely to have been smaller.

It may be assumed that in building the Wall, with journeys of no more than 2 or 3 miles, the Romans were able to move 2-ton loads as a matter of course. If the figure for the *angaria* can be increased to 2 tons, then the same proportional increase (4.15) ought to be permissible for the other vehicles.

The figures suggested in the table below allow for the heaviest wagons to carry the more exceptional 2-ton loads, say four or five pier stones or 70 walling stones, and for the *raeda* to carry two or three pier stones or about 45 walling stones. This seems to be more in keeping with the practical requirements of the army than the theoretical figures given in the *Theodosian Code*.

TYPE	KG	LB	TONS	
Angaria	2033	4480	2.00	4-wheeled wagon (oxen)
Raeda	1360	2995	1.34	4-wheeled wagon (oxen/mules)
Carrus	680	1498	0.67	2-wheeled cart (mules)

Table 4 Calculated revised capacity of vehicles

ACCESS ROADS

Wheeled transport needs some kind of road unless the weather is arid and the natural surface is reasonably smooth and hard. Iron tyres are more of a problem than pneumatic, the width and deformation of the latter considerably reducing the ground pressure. 'Road' does not in this context necessarily mean a properly engineered permanent way, but hollows, holes, and soft areas have to be made up with rough metalling. One should expect to find that the Military Way (see below) had a flimsy and intermittent predecessor, at the least on the approaches to all milecastles and forts. However, it should be noted that excavations at MC39 found no trace of a track between the later Military Way and the milecastle, although wheeled transport must have been used for transport of the stones of the gate piers. It may be of course that when that milecastle was under construction the weather was hot and dry which might obviate the need for any metalling.

In building the Wall the use of numerous *ad hoc* small quarries close to the line of the Wall and the large number of individual building sites would have made the installation of properly made roads, leading directly to all parts, prohibitive in terms of time and labour. But wheeled transport must have been used to carry all stones and other materials which were too heavy to make a balanced load for a pack animal.

THE MILITARY WAY

The Military Way (not to be confused with the modern Military Road) appears to have been built on the return from the Antonine Wall in the 160s. Therefore, although not a feature of the original design of Hadrian's Wall, a brief discussion will be useful to judge whether it may have been founded on an earlier service track used in building the Wall.

The road runs mostly less than 100yds behind the Wall and only in a few places, such as King's Hill (NY797693) and from MC 41-42, does it run as far as 200yds to the south. This would give a reasonably good route for materials along the line, but access to this route is restricted by the cliffs to the north and the steep ascents from the south, and it has unnecessarily severe gradients which must limit the utility of the line for wheeled construction traffic.

In at least one place it makes an extraordinary effort to stay close to the Wall. As the Military Way climbs up the rocky slope to the east from Peel Gap it turns sharply to the north in a cutting through a rock outcrop, as though to reach a more level gradient in the shortest time or to stay as close as possible to the Wall line. Diverting a little way to the south around the outcrop would have given a longer but much more gentle gradient at the cost of a slightly greater distance from the line. The modern farm track is briefly on the line of the Military Way as it crosses Peel Gap, but immediately to the east it takes a very much easier line to the south, and rejoins the Military Way just to the west of MC39. The labour of making the cutting seems excessive for a temporary track for servicing a building project, although the line may have been revised when the permanent road was built.

A little to the east of MC39, the Military Way climbs steeply with a sharp northward turn on the east side of Sycamore Gap; again, a relatively small diversion to the south would have reduced the gradient considerably and the same applies at other points. One wonders in fact whether the road was built with wheeled traffic in mind.

Bruce (1851, 75) had similar doubts '… the steepness of the road in some places is such, that most of our modern carmen … would be greatly puzzled if required to traverse it with a wagon laden with military stores'. He also notes that the carriers who used the Military Way before the building of the Military Road in the mid-eighteenth century used packhorses and not wheeled carriages. Wilmott notes the lack of wear on the southern portal of the *porta principalis sinistra* at Birdoswald and casts doubt on the volume of wheeled traffic on the Military Way. There are no wheel ruts in the thresholds of the west gate at Housesteads, showing that wheeled traffic did not leave the fort to go west along the Military Way; the only wheel ruts at this fort are at the east gate, and presumably derive from deliveries coming on the branch road running up from the Stanegate to the south-east.

The Military Way does not appear to be relevant to a construction track used during the building of the Wall, and was not constructed for use by wheeled traffic.

8

BUILDING OPERATIONS

As was shown in chapter 1, the line chosen for the wall ran through countryside which was largely cleared or cultivated, but in part more or less lightly wooded, with denser thickets in the valleys. These had to be cleared both for a working area and to give a clear line of sight either side of the wall. Gangs would have been at work along most of the length of the Wall at the same time and there would have been an 80-mile long corridor of building sites.

Tree felling was well within the experience of the legionary, as is shown on Trajan's Column (e.g. scene lxxiii) along with ground clearance and other building operations. The sort of work shown in this scene is precisely what would have been required for preparing the ground in advance of building operations in the wooded areas.

LAYING THE FOUNDATION AND FOOTINGS

The simple work of foundation-laying could have been carried out by any available soldier under suitable supervision. A shallow trench was dug, in the case of the Broad Wall sometimes involving no more than removal of the turf, and into this flags or large stones were bedded in clay or earth. The clay has often been referred to as 'puddled' but this is a technical term for forming a waterproof clay layer for ponds or canals whereas on the Wall clay was used simply in place of mortar for bonding stones.

On top of the Broad Wall foundation one to four courses of facing stones was laid as the footings: above this the Wall was reduced to its finished width by means of an offset on each face. The footings could be regarded as part of the foundation, although they would more conveniently have been laid by the curtain-wall builders who were dealing with large quantities of facing stones.

Laying the foundations was very different work, and used slabs rather than facing stones. It would thus be entirely logical for the footing courses to have been built by the curtain-wall builders.

The question of which gang laid the courses below the offset is important in relation to the allocation of curtain and structures to particular legions. Two legions, A and B, built with a single course (Standard A), legion C with three, or sometimes four, courses (Standard B) below the offset. If the courses below the offset were laid by the legion which laid the foundation, they do not indicate which legion built the superstructure, which is where the centurial stones come from; they might be one and the same legion, but they might well not be.

There are a number of points where the Narrow Wall was built on the Broad foundation, and in many cases this Broad foundation still carries one to three courses of broad footings. Between MC48 and T48b there is only a tiny piece of Broad Wall proper, consisting of six stones of the first course above the Standard B offset, and yet the Broad footing courses can be seen over most of this distance. It could be that the footings were built by gangs from the curtain-wall builders, preparing for the curtain wall to be carried up from the foundation, but it is not impossible that these courses were laid by the foundation builders.

The foundations and footings seem to have been built chiefly with clay as a bonding medium throughout. In his cross-section of the Wall near St Oswald's (Wall-mile 25) Warburton notes that 'what is underground is in clay' (50). He seems to be referring to the Broad footings. The evidence for the use of clay in the footings, as against the general use of mortar to bond the facing stones in the wall proper, does rather suggest the work of the foundation gangs.

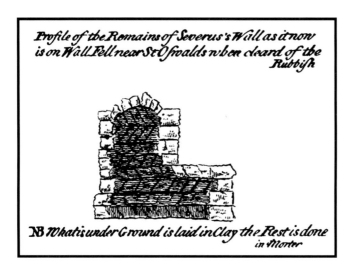

Left: 50 Warburton's cross-section of Hadrian's Wall near MC26

Opposite: 51 Different treatments of Narrow Wall on Broad Wall foundations

On the other hand, at T34a there were no footings in place when the building of the turret began, which ought to indicate that the footings were normally laid by the builders of the curtain wall and turrets.

Something of the sequence of building can be seen between T48a and T48b. The Narrow Wall here is built sometimes directly onto the broad foundation, behind one or two courses of broad footing, and sometimes onto the broad core at the level of the top of the second broad footing course. The broad-footing builders were clearly filling-in the core as they built. Equally, it is clear that at least two courses of footing could be built without any core between the faces (51). Excavations in the garden of the former Vicarage at Gilsland showed that the core of the Broad and Narrow footings was contemporary, indicating that the core of the former had not yet been laid before the gauge was reduced.

It seems in the present state of knowledge that there can be no certainty as to who built the footings. The evidence tends to suggest that they were the work of the curtain-wall gangs, but stronger evidence will be needed before the question can be finally settled.

BUILDING THE CURTAIN WALL

Once the foundations had been built, the laying of the facing stones was a simple business which could be taught to any legionary within the hour; of course speed and efficiency would come only with experience, but reasonable dexterity could be expected within a few days. An outline of the operations will make this point clear.

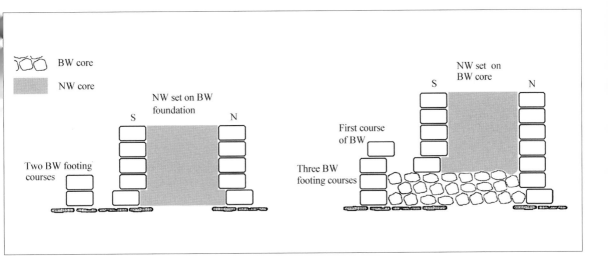

A mortar bed, the thickness of which called for more judgement than any other operation, although this need not have been particularly accurate, had to be laid on the preceding course with a trowel and the stone placed in position. The very roughness of the stone dressing called for only approximation in the laying, as the lack of a sharp arris marking the transition from face to joint made exactitude both impossible and unnecessary (52 and 53).

Above: 52 North wall of MC37

Left: 53 An ashlar wall, its appearance marred by damaged stones and uneven joints

Opposite above: 54 The first stage in building the curtain wall

Opposite below: 55 The second stage in building the curtain wall

The roughly squared rubble can be positioned to the nearest 5 or 10 millimetres without looking out of place, using a thump of a hammer to bed it down onto the mortar (or clay) and to correct any major misalignment. The tapered joints of many of the facing stones, though they may well have helped in 'bonding to the core' also had the advantage of always providing plenty of clearance between the stones however rough the dressing had been. Once the stone was in position it remained only to fill the joint between it and the previous stone, an operation made easier by the tapering joints which would allow mortar to fall easily to the bottom of the joint in successive trowelfuls until the joint was filled solid. It should be noted that clay alone was certainly used for bonding the facing stones of the Narrow Wall in Wall-mile 1. The facing stones would probably have been fixed to a line (a stretched string), making it unnecessary for the fixers to check for alignment and plumb.

As soon as two or three courses of facing stones had been laid it would be necessary to back them up with corework before proceeding higher, as the roughly squared rubble would hardly have been stable without it. The facing stones must have been built up equally at each side, requiring a pair of gangs working each side of the Wall. The core consists of rubble, sandstone along much of the wall, mostly whinstone over the crags, sometimes with clay or earth, sometimes with mortar, and sometimes dry.

The Wall could have been built up at each end of the gang-length to the height of the first scaffold lift, as shown by the dotted lines in *figure 54*; this would be eight courses, given the average size of stones.

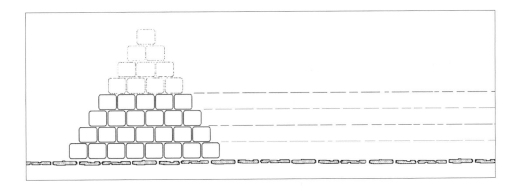

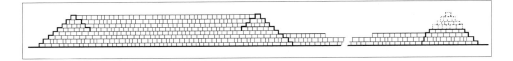

The height of 1470mm (58in) (185mm/7.25in x 8) is about right for the first lift of scaffolding, and the facing stones could not be lifted and laid at more than shoulder height even by two men. However, the ends of the core would have to be built up rather carefully if it were not to collapse, and it is more likely that the ends were build up in two stages of four courses each with a height of 735mm (29in). The stepped end of the core, reinforced by large stones running through the Wall at Willowford Bridge, presumably represents this method of working. Once the two ends were complete, the intervening gap could be filled very quickly course by course (55).

THE MILECASTLES

Milecastle walls

The milecastle walls were built in the same manner as the curtain wall and, at least in the original plan, to approximately the same gauge; the techniques of building these were broadly the same as the curtain wall. It was with corners, gateways, and towers that a different range of skills was called for and presented, for unskilled or semi-skilled builders, problems which are both different and more complex. When erecting the walls of a building it is normal to build up the corners first with a raking joint, to as great a height as possible, establishing both alignment and plumb. It is probable that the corners would be built by gang members who had at least a modicum of experience although this need not have been great. Once the corners are built it would be a simple matter to complete the wall in between by a less skilled gang, in the same way as lengths of curtain wall.

The external southern angles of the milecastles are invariably rounded rather than square, and the known internal angles are all square to the east of MC47. There is no structural reason for making the southern external corners rounded. However, when building a square external angle each side of the corner has to be plumbed; movement of one side of the stone may displace the other and the corner can quickly lean to one side. These errors have to be corrected and the building can be time consuming and slow. Furthermore, a supply of stones dressed on two faces is needed to form the quoins.

A rounded corner is easier to build when using unskilled labour and calls for less in the way of organisation and stone dressing. Once the first course of the curve has been set out, a job which can be done by eye in squared rubble, the wall builders have only to follow the course below and check that it is plumb on the one face. There is no need for quoin stones, and the whole corner can be built with ordinary walling stones. The fact that the stones were generally worked to a taper would have made building a curve much easier than building with parallel-sided stones.

Internal square corners are easier to build than external ones. Each wall has to be built on the correct line and plumbed, and alternate courses have to be lapped in order to achieve a tie, but adjustment of a stone on one face will not affect the other to any extent. Again, no specially dressed stones are needed, although it is easier if the faces do not project excessively. There is no obvious reason for MCS 47 and 48 and all the known replacement stone milecastles in the turf wall sector being rounded on their internal southern angles. They might have proved slightly easier to build than square angles, but it may equally be due to an unknown change in design.

The northern angles are simply right-angled junctions with the curtain wall of Hadrian's Wall. This, incidentally, indicates that the designers were not thinking in terms of joining a series of fortlets by a curtain wall, but were adding the milecastles to the Wall. This is in distinction to the forts, which have rounded northern angles even where they do not project, presumably because they were built to existing standard plans.

Milecastle gateways

It is worth looking at the building of the gateways in some detail, taking MC37 as a model. The piers of the north gate have five courses above the foundation, including the impost cap, with two stones to each course.

The hoisting and fixing of large stones is a relatively slow business – perhaps three or four stones per hour at most rather than one every two minutes as with the facing stones. Because of the closeness of the joints, probably 3-4mm, the mortar bed had to be carefully judged, mortar spread on the vertical joint of the previous stone and the stone lifted, positioned and lowered. In dry weather the stone has to be wetted to reduce the suction in the stones; if the suction is too great the mortar can become crumbly and sandy before the stone is bedded down, and it will not squeeze out a little as it ideally should.

Unlike building with walling stones, a scaffold would not be necessary for building up the large, squared stones of the gate piers. Here the weight is taken by the derrick and all the mason has to do is to guide it into place; there is no reason why this cannot be done with the aid of a ladder or two stones and a plank, and one may expect the building of the piers to proceed to the height of the impost caps without scaffolding. Indeed, scaffolding could have been a positive hindrance.

Once the stone was released from the lifting tackle, final adjustments would almost certainly be needed. With such stones it is often easiest to stand on the top bed while swinging a heavy (preferably wooden) hammer against face or bed to adjust either the horizontal position or any vertical inclination. In many places, where a course is inset from the one below, small slots were cut in the lower stone, apparently to take the toe of a pinch bar as an aid to moving the position of the upper stone.

To erect an arch, the voussoirs are built up on a timber formwork, known as a centre, which must be supported at the level of the springing line (56). This is one function of the projecting impost caps; the overhang is easily massive enough to carry the whole weight of the centre and the arch.

In fact, most of the weight of the arch is carried by that part of the cap which rests on the piers, rather than by the centre resting on the overhang of the cap (57). For this reason the centre does not have to be a massive structure and it is often a surprisingly lightweight affair.

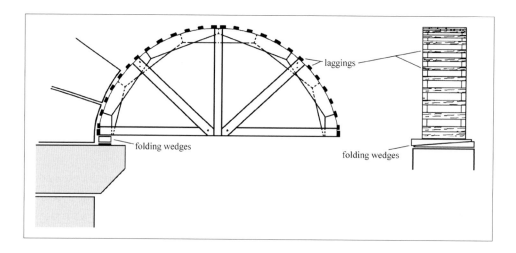

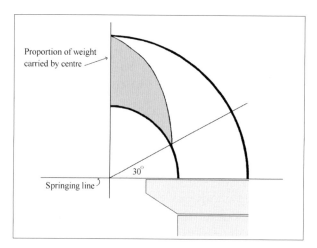

Above: 56 Typical centre, suitable for a milecastle or fort gateway

Left: 57 The loading on a centre

The centre rests not directly on its supports, but on folding wedges. As soon as the arch is complete the wedges are eased out to allow the centre to drop. There is no need to wait until the mortar is set; indeed it is advantageous to allow the weight of the voussoirs to settle as soon as possible to consolidate the mortar joints. The voussoirs in Roman military construction have tolerably well worked beds, and mortar has a comparatively small part to play in the stability of such an arch. It is a traditional saying in the masonry trade that mortar serves to keep the stones apart and to transmit the pressure evenly rather than to stick them together. Any inequalities are best dealt with by letting the mortar squeeze out from below the high spots while still soft. Once the centre is clear of the *soffit* of the arch the centre can be slid sideways, without disturbing the arch, as it serves no further purpose. It takes a matter of minutes rather than hours or months.

It is often said that a centre must be left in place until the mortar has set, as the arch will collapse without it. This is true for shallow arches, with a depth of ring of less than 10 per cent of the radius, but at MC37, with a radius of 1500mm (60in) and an average depth of voussoirs of 600mm (24in) the ratio is 40 per cent. As milecastle arch rings each weigh about 2.8 tonnes, the action of fixing the walling stones around them would not have had the slightest effect on the arch. Milecastle arches will stand alone without the slightest danger of collapse.

As shown by the lewis holes in all the surviving voussoirs, the stones were put in place with the aid of a derrick. With an average weight of around 283kg (624lb) it would not be possible to place them by hand.

The differing spans of front and rear arches in gateway types II/IV was noted in chapter 2. The variation is some 300-450mm (12-18in), and only by adding 150-225mm (6-9in) thick extra laggings to the centre for the front arch could it have been used for the rear arch. It is also probable that the centre would have been too small to be supported on the impost caps of the wider arch, and additional, ground-based, support for the centre would have been needed. The alternative would have been the use of a second centre of the appropriate size. Whatever solution was adopted, considerable additional labour was needed simply to provide a wider rear arch, for which no material advantage can be seen. It is possible that an arch was not provided at the rear of type II/IV gateways, but a timber lintel used instead.

Unlike the piers, scaffolding would be desirable for the building of the arches, but this need have been no more than a simple trestle.

It will be appreciated that the work of building a gateway is a different specialisation from other work on the Wall, and would have been the responsibility of separate, specialist gangs. It would be desirable for the gate-building gang to complete the building of the arch immediately following completion of the piers, rather than having to return at a later date (58).

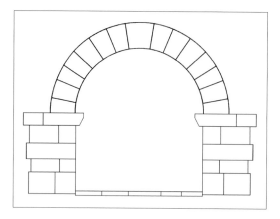

58 A milecastle gate: the work of a specialist gang

Where evidence is available, the north gates and north walls of the milecastles seem to have been built up in advance of the side walls. Examples where this is clear are MCS 9, 13, 17, 18, 19, 20, 22, 27, 41 and 42. For a convenient summary of the evidence see Hunneysett 1980. The north walls may have been built at the same time as the gateways, the wall builders following the raising of the piers course by course. It would, however, not be convenient to have a wall-building gang working at the same time as the pier builders and there is no reason why wall-building could not have been delayed until the piers were fully built. Although the outer (i.e. east and west) faces of the piers often have upper courses projecting over lower ones, the stones are massive enough to be stable without additional support.

The towers of the milecastle gateways present the same problems as the turrets.

Turrets

Turrets are relatively complex structures, and building them was not a simple operation. Square corners and openings for doors and windows are significantly more difficult to build than simply putting one stone on top of another to build a long length of wall. The square corners will have taken a degree of skill and care if the turret walls were to be more or less vertical. On the ground floor the provision of a doorway will have added to the skill needed, with a square end to two of the side walls to form the door jambs. At the higher levels windows, the number of which is unknown, will have called for building jambs and perhaps arched heads. If, as has been suggested, the walls were reduced in thickness above Wall-top height (Hill 1997), the offset will have to have been provided for. There would thus have been comparatively little straightforward walling to be done on a turret. The gangs responsible for the work on a turret will have needed a significantly greater degree of skill and experience than those building the curtain wall.

The purpose of the wing walls was to allow the curtain wall to bond with the turret by means of a raking joint. The length of the wing walls suggests that building to full height was initially provided for but it is almost certain that practical logistics of scaffolding would have dictated otherwise. The quantity of scaffolding needed to build a turret or tower (chapter 5) makes it highly unlikely that any such structure was built to a height of more than 4-5ft (1200-1500mm) or so in advance of the completion of the curtain wall.

Building towers as part of a curtain wall was not new: interval towers in stone-walled forts were part of the army's experience. At Housesteads there was good evidence that the towers had been built before the curtain wall, and there is similar evidence for the early erection of gate towers at Greatchesters. However, in a fort the maximum distance between towers is 37m (40yds), and it would be a comparatively simple matter to move the scaffolding by man-carry from tower to tower. But in the case of the Wall turrets the effort needed to move 7 tons of scaffolding 540yds over often difficult ground was quite another matter.

The probable procedure adopted was for the several milecastle gateway and turret gangs to precede the curtain builders to begin the building of each structure both in order to mark the site and because of the level of skill needed. This procedure was certainly followed on the Antonine Wall, as shown by the excavation of Seabegs fortlet. In view of the surviving stonework at T34a, it is worth looking at the way in which the work was actually carried out.

As usual the corners would be built first, taking up a good part of the external wall of a turret and even more of the internal walls (59). As suggested for the curtain wall, this lowest stage may have been built in two phases. The footing course of the wing walls would also be laid. At T34a, a Standard A turret, only part of the footing course of the wing wall was laid (dark shading in *figure 60*, which is a diagrammatic representation of the existing bonding), and on that was built part of the first course of the wall proper, and probably the second.

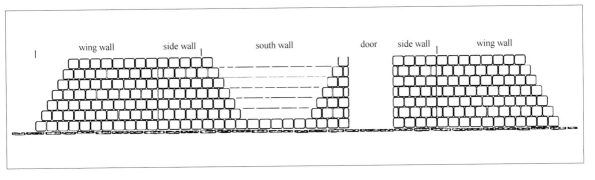

wing wall   side wall   south wall   door   side wall   wing wall

59 The first stage in building the lower part of a turret

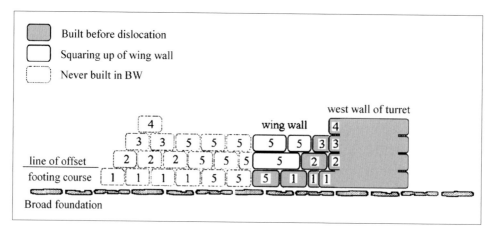

60 T34a west wing wall. The numbers show the logical sequence of work

This sequence is the most likely as the squaring-off of the wing wall, following the reduction in gauge, takes in the footing course and two more. Each succeeding course added to the turret wall would have necessitated adding one more stone to the preceding course of the wing wall. It is not easy to think of a more inefficient way of building. It may be that the gang building the turret were doing no more than laying the first three or four courses before handing over to another gang to complete the building, and that the second gang did not arrive on site until after the reduction in gauge.

Apart from materials, which would have to be taken to the site anyway, the turret builders would have only themselves to move from site to site. Any signs of occupation in turrets which were demolished (as the result of the fort decision) before the curtain wall reached them cannot be taken as indicating that they were ever completed. On building sites today the existence of two walls meeting at right angles provides shelter for breaks, and it must be assumed that human nature has remained unchanged.

The milecastle towers were considerably smaller plan than the turrets, and the building of the corners will have taken up all the side walls and most of the front and back walls. As with the turrets, windows, perhaps doors leading on to the curtain wall, and possibly a doorway leading to a balcony, were also needed.

FORTS

This section looks at the nature of the work entailed in building the curtain wall, towers, and gateways, and does not include the internal buildings.

The walls around forts were significantly thinner than the curtain of the Wall but the practicalities of building them were identical to those of building the Wall.

Interval towers

The techniques of building the towers were no different from the turrets. Both were built of squared rubble, both had doors, windows, floors, and roofs. They were similarly complex structures and begun in advance of the outer wall, complete with wing walls. This was not because the Romans saw them necessarily as distinct structural units but because that is the most convenient way to build, just as the turrets and milecastles were begun before the curtain wall.

The gateways

In many respects the gateways of the forts present similar problems to those of the milecastles. They have in common the large, squared stones of the piers and the worked voussoirs, and dressing the stones for the piers and arches of the fort gateways was a similar process to that required for the milecastles, although with some added complications. On the milecastle gateways the length of the stones of the outer sides of both piers could be of variable length (marked as 'unmeasured' on *figure 61*). Putting two such gateways together to form the twin portals of the fort gateways meant that what was in effect a conjoined central pier had to be of definite dimensions to form the central pier, or *spina*. The difference in working would not be great, but the size of the *spina* had to be determined and the stones worked to suit.

The arches of the gateways called for exactly the same techniques in building as those of the milecastle. The difference in span of front and rear arches in type II/IV milecastle gateways was noted earlier; the same problem applies to the gateways of Housesteads fort which have no projecting inner piers.

The major difference between the milecastle and fort gateways lies in the superstructure. Whereas the former have small, simple towers, the latter have substantial upper storeys, with towers at either side of the portals and probably some superstructure above the portals as exemplified by the reconstruction at South Shields (*8*). The overall width, including the towers, was twice that of two milecastle gateways.

Despite the size and sophistication there was no call for any techniques of construction different from those required for the milecastle gateways.

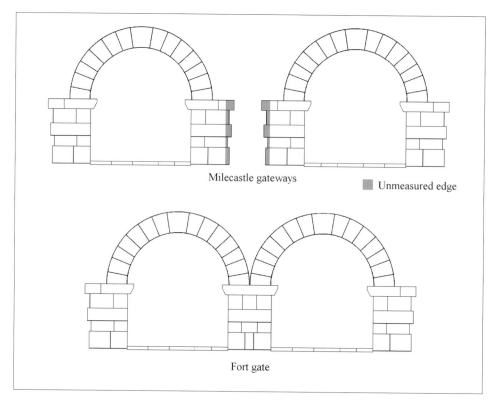

Milecastle gateways

■ Unmeasured edge

Fort gate

61 A comparison between milecastle and fort gate arches

SPECIALISATION

'Turret gangs' have been referred to as a separate force, and one would expect specialised gangs to be building turrets as the work was more skilled, and called for more experience, than building the curtain. The same is true of the gateways which would very probably have been built by yet another gang as the work of building in massive solid stone is very different from building with squared rubble and called for a degree of skill which was not necessary for curtain building. Skilled legionaries must have been at a premium in such a huge enterprise, and to make best use of the available men one may suspect that there were separate gangs engaged in building foundations, turrets and towers, gateways, and curtain wall. It is doubtful if they were ever interchangeable other than by the 'promotion' of individuals as the result of experience.

The building of scaffolding would ideally also have been the work of specialist gangs, although it is possible that this could have been carried out by the building gangs.

THE DITCH AND VALLUM

Digging the ditch was one part of the work with which every Roman legionary would have been familiar, such activities being a part of their training (Vegetius I.4 and I.21; Davies 1989, Chap V). It was a straightforward matter of excavation with *dolabra* and spade, shovelling the earth into baskets to be hauled out and dumped as a glacis, and raked level, although in places along the Wall it was left in heaps (e.g. Wall Fell and Appletree). A ditch of these proportions, with the sides at an angle to the horizontal of about 33°, has something in common with a small road cutting, and as such British army methods may be usefully applied, thus: 'to dig small trenches at each side along the cut lines at ground level at each side, and to take off the soil in between in layers of about 1ft in depth, commencing each layer 1ft nearer the centre line at each side. By this means stepped sides will be formed, which can be dressed to the required slope' (War Office 1935, 95). Whether the Roman builders used precisely this method cannot be established, but it, or something on similar lines, would certainly be more satisfactory than trying to form the finished profile of the ditch as work proceeded.

The presence of the ditch would have interfered seriously with the movement of materials from any quarries to the north of the wall, and ideally it would have been planned as the last part of the programme to be carried out. The unfinished state of the ditch at Limestone Corner may indicate that it did indeed fall late in the sequence after any initial enthusiasm had evaporated.

The only gap along the crags where, so far as is known, the ditch was not dug, is at Housesteads. It may be no coincidence that the only quarry definitely known to be north of the Wall, along the crags, was at Queen's Crag to the north-east of Housesteads, as well as at points between Queen's Crag and the Wall.

Premature digging of the Vallum, too, would also have been a considerable nuisance to the builders. The limiting of access from the south to roughly 7-mile intervals would have added insult to injury for men already called on to add forts to a project of which they had probably already had enough.

9

ORGANISATIONAL ASPECTS OF THE WORK

THE BUILDING SEASON AND WORKING WEEK

Two climatic factors affect building work: rain and frost. Heavy rain can be a more serious event than frost. Heavy rain against the face of new work is liable to wash out unset mortar, and remaining mortar will be weakened as excess water causes lime to leach out. Rain would prevent building work continuing, but there are surprisingly few days on which the weather is too bad for outdoor work by men accustomed to it. Light drizzle can usually be ignored.

Working stone is affected by rain in two ways. First, hammers will tend to slip from the head of the tool causing injury. Secondly, rain forms the resulting dust into a paste which makes it near impossible to see what is being done. The problem can be avoided by the provision of simple overhead shelters.

The factor which has an immediately damaging effect, but occurs at reasonably well-fixed seasons of the year, is frost, which affects mortar by freezing any uncombined water and disrupting the partially formed crystalline structure. The harder the frost, the greater the depth to which unset mortar will be affected. The effect of moderate frosts can be mitigated by covering new work with straw, bracken, or other suitable materials until the frost has lifted or the mortar has set.

As discussed in the Introduction, the consensus tends towards the view that when the Wall was built the climate resembled that of today. Building work can now normally be carried out from the beginning of March to the end of October without serious risk of frost damage, and in the second century the position is likely to have been no more restricted. This gives a notional season of about 35 weeks, or 245 days, for building with lime mortar.

It cannot be supposed that the troops worked continuously throughout this period, and some allowance must be made for rest days, festivals, and other public holidays. The seven-day week was known in Rome by the time of Augustus, but the seventh day was not a day of rest until the conversion of the empire to Christianity. The fragmentary third-century *Feriale Duranum* shows 46 festivals (Fink 1971, No. 117), and it is reasonable to assume at least the same number for the second century. Taking a slightly arbitrary figure of 45 days of rest leaves a season of 200 days, coinciding with the estimate given by Robert Rawlinson of 200 working days in a year permitted by the weather in the Wall area (Bruce 1851). This equates to working just under six days out of seven.

The working day might reasonably be taken as eight effective hours; this excludes time for rest and refreshment, and for marching to and from the temporary camps. A total of, say, 10 hours away from camp is not excessive, and during the season suggested there is sufficient daylight for this to be possible.

Provided the weather was not too bad for the legionaries to continue to live in tents, it is possible that some work may have continued during at least part of the October-March period. Digging of the ditch and Vallum was certainly possible in dry periods which were free of hard frosts. Transport of prepared walling stones could easily have been carried out in the absence of rain (which would have turned the tracks into quagmires). Quarrying is not normally carried out in the winter, as there is an increased chance of newly quarried blocks being damaged by frost before they have dried out. Blocks which had already been quarried could have been worked into walling stones or pier stones; simple shelters would have allowed this work to be continued over most of the year.

Against this scenario must be balanced the unhappiness of legionaries living in tents over part of the winter while auxiliaries (unless they were involved in the building) were living in well-built barracks with families and friends close by.[1]

Much speculation is inherent in this discussion of the working season. For how many days in the season were the men actually available for work? Was the effective working day of six, eight or ten hours (which suggests an overall day of something approaching eight, ten, and twelve hours respectively)? Did the legions return to winter quarters, and if so, how long did they spend there?

All that can be done is to take note of the above points, and suggest around 200 days, working eight hours a day, as a realistic estimate for building work and rather more for other works.

THE LABOUR FORCE

In order to make an assessment of the possible labour force present during the building of the Wall, it is necessary to look for evidence of what units, or types of unit, were involved. A judgement will be made as to the possible total manpower engaged on the project: it is unlikely that this can ever be more than a rough approximation.

The evidence of inscriptions

The majority of inscriptions relating to the Wall were analysed in a very detailed paper by Stevens in 1966. The inscriptions are of two types. First, there are the few formal dedications from forts and milecastles, naming the emperor, the governor, and the unit responsible. Secondly there are hundreds of small inscriptions, records left by work gangs on the curtain wall and Vallum and in forts, which simply record the gang, normally a century, sometimes with the cohort and/or legion in addition. These inscriptions, known as centurial stones, are almost uniformly crudely cut, as befitted what were probably no more than temporary records.

The Wall and forts

The builders of forts were recorded in inscriptions set up over the gateways. Only three Hadrianic dedicatory inscriptions survive from fort gateways: Haltonchesters, legion IV, *RIB* 1427; Greatchesters, unit not named, *RIB* 1736; Moresby, legion XX, *RIB* 801.

Milecastle gateways carried smaller and less formal inscriptions, of which six survive: *RIB* 1634 (MC37), 1637, and 1638 (MC38) name legion II Augusta and the governor Platorius Nepos; this governor is also named on the fragmentary *RIB* 1666 (MC42) which is very similar in style to the previous three and was almost certainly the work of legion II; *RIB* 1852 (probably MC47) names legion XX (but not the governor), and *RIB* 1935 (MC50TW) is a wooden fragment, on which the name of the unit does not survive although Nepos does appear to be named. A fragmentary inscription found at Vindolanda, *RIB* 1702 is so similar to those from MCS 37 and 38 that it may have been carried there from the Wall in modern times. The fact that legion VI is not recorded as building milecastles does not mean that they did not do so; there is a severe paucity of milecastle inscriptions and there are three designs of gateways.

It may be assumed that each legion was present for the same length of time and in the same numbers throughout the building programme. It is probable that legion IX had left the province at some point before the Wall was built, and legions II Augusta, VI Victrix, and XX Valeria Victrix are seen as the legionary garrison of the province during Wall building. All three legions are recorded building the curtain wall and turrets.

It was not only the legions which had some involvement in building the forts; the only certain Hadrianic dedication from an internal building of a fort, *RIB* 1340, found in the portico of the granary at Benwell, was put up by a detachment from the British Fleet, the *Classis Britannica*. The similarity in design of granaries at Rudchester and Haltonchesters has been held to suggest that the fleet may also have built those as well. The fleet is also recorded on two centurial stones from the Birdoswald area (*RIB* 1944, *RIB* 1945) which perhaps came from the rebuilding of the first 4 miles of the Turf Wall in stone, believed to have taken place later in Hadrian's reign. The fact that the fleet was involved in a relatively small building programme means that their involvement in similar work during the major campaign cannot be ruled out.

Auxiliary units are known to have been directly involved in building work before and during Hadrian's reign. Documents from Vindolanda and a Hadrianic dedication from Hardknott provide firm evidence of this, but there is no dated record of their involvement in the initial building of the Wall. There is an undated auxiliary cavalry building inscription from the line of the Wall just to the west of T26b, Brunton, and a similar one from Chesters fort. A stone from just east of the secondary tower at Willowford Bridge names a centurion with possible Dacian origins. As Chesters was garrisoned by cavalry under Hadrian and in the late second/early third century, and a Dacian cohort was stationed at Birdoswald, it is possible that all three stones refer to repair by units in garrison rather than to original building.

The Vallum

Auxiliaries dug at least a part of the Vallum. There are 16 inscriptions which are known, or suggested, to relate to the building of the Vallum. Of these, eight stones, *RIB* 1361, 1362, 1363, 1364, 1365, 1367, 1376, and *JRS* I 1960, 10, were all found on or close to one or other of the Vallum mounds. These all appear to relate to work by auxiliaries. It has been suggested that legionaries were also involved in digging the Vallum, but the evidence is unsafe and it seems likely that the whole of the Vallum was dug by auxiliaries.

The ditch

There is no evidence as to which units dug the ditch to the north of the Wall; it may have been auxiliaries, legions, or the fleet.

OTHER AUXILIARY AND NATIVE INVOLVEMENT

The auxiliaries may have taken part in ancillary aspects of the work, such as transport and fuel gathering, which would leave no epigraphic trace and for which there is no basis on which to make reasonable estimates. Similarly, the number of auxiliary units engaged on building the Vallum cannot be judged as only one unit is mentioned on the eight stones found in close association with the Vallum.

The engagement of the native population on some parts of the work cannot be ruled out. There are inscriptions referring to work by *civitates* (*RIB* 1672, 1673, 1843, 1844, 1962, 2022 and 2053) from some distance away but it is believed that these relate to later repairs. It is possible that local native labour may have been present as paid labourers, or suppliers of materials, or as forced levies,[2] but in the absence of any evidence it is not possible to make any estimate of numbers.

THE SIZE OF THE LEGIONARY LABOUR FORCE

Each legion consisted of 10 cohorts: II–X had 480 men in six centuries, but cohort I had been increased to 800 men, divided into five double centuries, in the late first century. This brought the total in a legion to 5120. There is some uncertainty about the size of cohort I in the first half of the second century and for the purpose of this exercise it will be taken as 480 men giving a total of 4800 in a legion.

Stevens believed that each century built in 20ft lengths, giving a cohort length of 120ft, and that each sub-unit placed a centurial stone at each end of its piece of work. The stones were placed on both sides of the Wall and, as has been shown, the Wall would have been built in at least three horizontal 'layers'. Taking the stone Wall from Wallsend to the Irthing, 49 Roman miles, there should have been around 47,500 centurial stones, of which around 1 per cent survive. Given this small number, and the fact that the majority come from the central sector where the Wall has survived best, the sample is too small to provide any statistical basis for estimating how much work was done by a given cohort, and which cohorts were present.

There is another problem with centurial stones. The division of work into both horizontal and vertical blocks means that a single centurial stone lying in tumbled ruins gives no indication of what part that unit was responsible for. Centurial stones, as will be emphasised again, are evidence for the builders of the Wall immediately adjacent to them, and for nothing else.

Some men must have been left as a garrison in the legionary bases of York, Chester, and Caerleon, if only to prevent theft and to carry out routine maintenance; one cohort per legion might be a reasonable assumption. It is unlikely that training and similar military affairs would have been forgotten, and it might be allowed that at all times the equivalent of one further cohort per legion was engaged in such activities. This leaves a maximum of eight cohorts per legion, or 144 centuries, available for building the Wall. The cohorts would presumably be rotated between training, building, and garrison duties.

It might be assumed that the legions were up to establishment strength and that 80 men per century were nominally available, but it is not normal in modern armies for military units to be at their paper strengths. It is difficult to know what allowance to make for any shortages but it is possible to give an indication of what the situation might have been.

The modern British army is about 8 per cent under-strength in infantry soldiers, and of those nominally present about 1 per cent are absent without leave; applying this to the Roman century gives an actual strength of about 73 men which will be used as the basis for the following calculations. These and other subtractions are summarised in *Table 5*.

Men who were trained as clerks, technicians, and other specialists were *immunes*, not required to carry out fatigues. Breeze (1969) argues that at a conservative estimate 'the administrative staff and technicians' of the legion amounted to over 600 men, spread throughout the legion. A figure of 10 men per century unavailable for building work seems to be a reasonably safe figure to use.

There is little evidence for the proportion of men on leave at any one time, but perhaps two men per century might be a reasonable estimate.

Some men will have been on the sick list. No records of legions' sickness rates are available, but there is one from an auxiliary unit in Britain: the strength report of *cohors I Tungrorum* at Vindolanda in the early years of the second century (Bowman 1994). The roll carries 752 men of whom 296 were actually at Vindolanda and of the latter 31, or 10.5 per cent, were on the sick list. If it can be assumed that this rate applied to the whole unit, and that the sickness rate in a legion would be roughly the same, then the century of 73 would lose about 8 men.

It is known that legionaries served on the staff of the provincial governor, and some were sent out on various duties connected more with the administration of the province than with the work of the legion; some allowance for absence on these duties must be made. The majority of such duties might be awarded to the cohort left at base, but some would come from those cohorts engaged in building. It would have been sensible to use some of the *immunes* for this work, but perhaps one man per century could be allowed for this element; this is shown in the table as 'official duties'.

In all armies of all ages there has been a strong tendency for soldiers to engage themselves on more interesting, or even theoretical, duties not directly related to the tedious task in hand, finding specious reasons which would satisfy all but the most searching enquiry ('carrying a clipboard and looking busy'). It is difficult to estimate the numbers who might have found themselves such employment; a minimum figure might be one man in a century, listed as 'non-official' duties.

While building the Wall the troops were based in temporary camps, which could not be left unattended during the day. Apart from the tents there would be food stores and reserves of tools, as well as personal possessions, and some guards would be needed to counter casual theft from both opportunist civilians and light-fingered soldiers. In a camp for two cohorts, perhaps one man per century, in addition to any available walking wounded, might be so employed

This gives a hypothetical figure for available manpower of 2400 men in 48 centuries in each of three legions, a total of 7200.

Establishment		80
Under-strength & AWL		7
Actual strength		73
Immunes	10	
On leave	2	
Sick/injured	8	
Official duties	1	
'Non-official' duties	1	
Camp duties	1	
Less		23
Final strength		50

Table 5 Actual strength of a century

HORIZONTAL BUILDING AND CENTURIAL LENGTHS

At the start of work, each unit, whether century or cohort, would build up sections of wall at the ends and perhaps also at intervals along their allocated length, and then fill-in up to the level of the first scaffold lift, a height of 1200–1500mm or so.

Unless scaffolding was immediately available, the gang which built the lower part would be obliged to move on to another section, leapfrogging within the legionary length; this would naturally divide the work into horizontal blocks. When returning with scaffolding, the order of work might be quite different, with century One building on the work of century Six, and so on, thus dividing the work into vertical blocks.

The likelihood is that at any one time a legionary length would have some parts built to full height, some built up to an intermediate height, some built to 1500mm (5ft), some just started, some with only the foundation put in, and some still virgin ground. These sections would not necessarily all be contiguous but would be scattered over the legionary or cohort length. Any disruption, be it war, rebellion, end of season, or temporary shortage of materials might well lead to completion by another unit, whether that unit was century, cohort, or legion.

What most certainly did not happen was that the Wall unrolled over the countryside as a full-height entity.

At the start and finish of a 'length' the Wall did not have a vertical end; successive courses would be stepped back up to the height to which that section had been built (62). If at full height, this raking joint would cover a horizontal distance of 2-3m (6-9ft) along the wall; the century completing the adjoining section might put their stone anywhere within the area of wall above the raking joint, or indeed to one side of it (63).

At T26b, Brunton, some Broad Wall was built to the west side of the

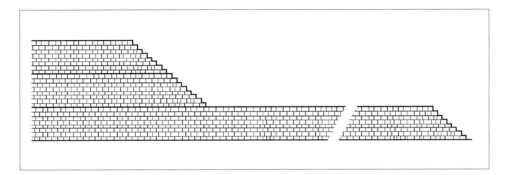

62 The end of a centurial length

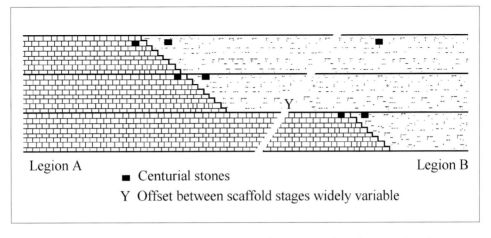

63 Alternative positions of centurial stones at the end of a century/cohort/legionary length

uncompleted turret. On the east side of the turret, the Broad wing wall reached only a height of some 900mm (3ft) and of the curtain only the foundation had been laid; the Broad Wall builders seem to have been coming downhill towards the turret and had reached Planetrees (about 800m (875yds) to the east) when the gauge of the Wall was narrowed. Again, it is most unlikely that more than the lowest few courses of Broad Wall had been built. The work may have been completed by a different legion, cohort, or century leading to a variety of 'signatures'; any attempt to build up a pattern of working using these stones would depend very much on which stones had been discovered. If legions A and B had each built up two lifts before dislocation, then a third legion could have built the third lift, introducing even more complications, as shown in *figure 64*.

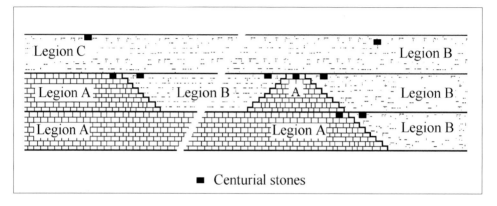

Above: 64 The likely effect of dislocation on the placing of centurial stones

Below: 65 Least likely appearance at the end of a centurial length

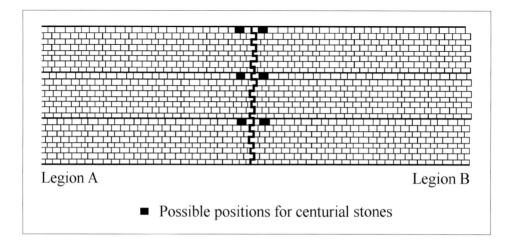

The work of different gangs will never have met with a vertical joints as shown in *figure 65*. To repeat, centurial stones are evidence for the work immediately around those stones and for nothing else.

It must not be forgotten that, while a considerable degree of organisation must have existed, work will not always have gone to plan. There will have been shortages of materials due to such factors as transport difficulties (sick or lame animals), shortage of lime (collapse of a kiln, difficulty in obtaining fuel, a poor 'burn'), shortage of stone (difficult beds in a quarry, need to open a new quarry), and so on. Disruptions in building the Wall may not have seriously held up the overall programme, as men could be moved to other work, but they would give rise to dislocation of the work in progress. Some signs of 'dislocation' may, in part at least, be due to these factors rather than widespread major dislocation due to a single cause.

It is not clear whether, at the junction of work between the elements of two legions or between two cohorts of the same legion, a stone recording that unit or sub-unit was always erected. Also, a stone recording the presence of a legion or a cohort must indicate no more than the presence of some members of that unit. Whether a centurial stone indicates that the whole of the century was present must also be uncertain. It may well be that a century might at times be divided between two sections of wall not immediately adjacent; whether in that case both sections would 'sign' their work is a matter of speculation.

It was argued above that the effective strength of a century might be no more than 50 men, and below it will be seen that the size of a gang engaged on actually building the Wall might be in the region of 30 men. If these figures are even approximately right, it suggests that centuries might be broken down into two building gangs, or that part of the century was quarrying or lime burning for a single building gang.

Stevens suggests that in Wall-mile 49-50 each century was responsible for a length of 20ft and a cohort for 120ft. This is very short, as a century could have completed its allotment in a very short time. However, this part of the Wall was rebuilt in stone after the rest of the Wall was completed, and perhaps timber was available to allow for very long lengths to have been scaffolded at once. This would allow a number of gangs to work alongside each other, and perhaps a large proportion of this mile was built simultaneously.

It has also been suggested that, assuming two legions were at work in the central sector, the length allocated to a century might have been 20m (22yds). But in the central sector it is clear that work was being completed after the decision to narrow the wall, and thus that this was not necessarily organised in the same way as in the original scheme.

It seems that in the present state of knowledge the question of centurial lengths must remain open.

RATE OF BUILDING

This is another very speculative area of study, as there are so many unknown factors involved. The rate at which stones could be laid in the Wall depends very much on the level of organisation, the methods of transport, the precise nature of the quarry from which stone was being extracted for a particular length of Wall, and the difficulty or otherwise in working the stone; to none of these can a wholly satisfactory answer be obtained.

In view of this, there will be no attempt to produce an overall timetable for the works. What will be offered is a theoretically possible rate, with appropriate labour force, at which building could have taken place under predetermined conditions. It will serve as an indication of what could have been done, but it would be very dangerous to multiply this up for the Wall as a whole.

The size of the facing stones varies considerably, with occasional instances of both very large and very small stones being used. On the whole, however, the statement in the *Handbook* that the stones are 'tolerably uniform' can be upheld. As a result of taking measurements at a number of points along the Wall, the author sees the typical size as 260 x 380 x 180mm (10.25 x 15 x 7in), and this has been used in the calculations of the rate of building. An allowance of 6mm (0.25in) for bed joints and 12mm (0.5in) for vertical joints has been made. This gives an overall size of stones including joints as 273 x 380 x 185mm (10.75 x 15 x 7.25in). This in turn gives an average figure of approximately 20 stones per square metre, or 17 per square yard, of facing.

The stones were generally tapered, and allowing a taper of 75mm (3in) on each of the two vertical joints, the typical stone will weigh about 29kg (64lb).

Curtain wall

The following outline assumes that the work is that of building the body of the broad curtain wall, and in reasonably easy country with good access.

One man, fit and used to the work, can lift a 64lb stone on his own, but the effort would soon lead to a serious slowing of the pace. It is not an unreasonable burden for two men working continuously, and it is here assumed that there were two men lifting stones from a heap, placing them on the wall, and adjusting their position. A third man would spread mortar for the bed and fill the joints after fixing. It is assumed that the joints would be roughly pointed as work proceeded. This would take well under two minutes per stone, giving a rate of 2yds per hour, with over 22 minutes to spare. This rate may seem very quick, but it ought to be easily within the capacity of three fit men with some experience, and is approximately the same as for modern large concrete block-work but with a more generous labour allowance. A team of three fixers would be able to interchange to give a variation between lifting and spreading mortar as work proceeded. It is assumed that the stones from the quarry would be dumped, or moved by others after dumping, within 5m of the working area.

Three men actually building are but a fraction of the numbers working in support. To maintain this rate of fixing, 4 men would be required for mixing mortar, 3 for filling the core, 4 to provide clay for bonding the core, with 1 man as a general labourer, bringing the total to 15. As both faces of the Wall have to be built up at the same time and the same rate, the total gang will be around 30 men. In practice this is probably too many, but the error is on the right side to give an indication of what could be done as a minimum with the available labour force.

Stone would be needed in large quantities to keep pace with the fixing gang. A not unreasonable estimate for quarrying and dressing stone for the facings is 45 men. A further 10 men would be needed to quarry core stone and break it into suitable pieces.

It must be understood that the above figures are no more than an example of how efficient, well-motivated gangs under good supervision might work in good weather on simple walling. It would be quite improper simply to multiply this up to arrive at a global figure for building the Wall. However, it may be justifiable to see what might happen if this rate of working were maintained for a period, and this will be done after looking at the labour force needed for milecastles and turrets.

Turrets and milecastles

The turrets and milecastles are even less easy to quantify than the curtain wall, but an attempt has been made. Although turret walls are much thinner than the curtain wall, the corners, door, and bonding with the wing walls means that work would be much slower for a given volume.

A gang of 15 men might build the north wall; as it was such a short length they could move from one side to another to build two or three courses at a time. Another gang, of seven men (three fixers, two mortar mixers, one for the small amount of core, and one labourer) could at the same time build the side walls. These 22 men could build the first four courses in 20 hours, or two and a half days; five days would see the turret built to a height of 58in (1470mm). This feels about right, but could well be too generous.

The reduced volume and speed would call for fewer quarrymen and dressers than the curtain wall. Quarrying and dressing walling stones is taken at half the rate for the curtain wall, reducing the number of men to 23. Much less core stone is needed, so little that perhaps three men would suffice. This brings the total for quarrying and dressing to 26 men, and the total labour involved in building a turret to 48 men.

Building the piers of a milecastle gateway might be at the rate of three stones an hour, using two men to fix, three on the derrick, one mortar mixer, and one labourer. Allowing for some problems, a rate of 20 stones a day would see the piers of one gate completed in no more than 2 days. Some time must be allowed for erecting the centre and trestles twice on each gate; one day would be generous. At the same rate of building as for the piers, the twin arches of a gate would take one and a half days. This brings the total to four and a half days; relaxing the rate a little, one gang of seven men might build the north and south gates of a milecastle in 10 days.

The time needed to quarry the stone for the milecastle gateways is a difficult area, as it depends very much on the nature of the quarry. Five quarrymen might take four days to produce the stone for both gateways. Another five might be needed to scapple the stones to the right size for the masons to begin working, and one labourer might be allowed.

The labour needed to work the piers and voussoirs of the milecastle gates might be estimated at 280 man-days for both gates. To this figure must be added the working of the less-exacting foundation blocks beneath the piers, say one man-day for each of two stones beneath each pier. This adds 16 man-days, total 296, for each milecastle: 30 men would take about 10 days to work the stone.

The labour force for all operations to build two milecastle gateways is: building gang 7, quarrymen 11, dressers 30, a total of 48 men.

Foundations

The foundations were usually laid in a very shallow trench; this would mean no more than digging out turf or cutting into the topsoil to perhaps 150mm (6in) deep with a width of just over 3m. Two men could dig one linear metre per hour without difficulty.

Spreading clay and laying flagstones along the edges might involve, at each side, one man spreading clay and two men laying the large slabs which average no more than three per metre. This could be done at the rate of at least 1m every quarter hour. Four men filling the centre of the foundation with clay and small stone could work at the same rate. To keep pace with this rate of laying, eight men would be needed on excavation, a total of 18 men which might be rounded up to 20 men laying 4m per hour.

Approximately 12 quarrymen and 6 stone breakers would be needed to keep up with the rate of laying. This brings the total foundation labour force to 38 men.

RATE FOR BUILDING A 'LEGIONARY LENGTH'

This section looks at how quickly the early stages of a legionary length of 5 miles could be built, given the same conditions as outlined above. Dimensions here are given in yards, following the traditional measurement of the length between turrets and milecastles.

The speed given there for building curtain wall uses a gang of 30 men backed up by 55 men quarrying and dressing the stone. These numbers could build one square yard in about half an hour; at an initial height of 735mm (29in), they would build at the rate of 20 linear yards in an 8-hour day.[3]

The nominal interval between turrets and milecastles is 540yds, referred to as a 'curtain'. The first four courses of a curtain would thus be completed in 27 gang-days.

Hooley and Breeze suggest 5 miles, 15 curtains, as a 'legionary block'; this would take 405 gang-days. If a legion allocated 1275 men, 15 complete gangs of builders and quarrymen, to building curtain wall, there would be three gangs to each mile, one to each curtain. The first four courses of a 5-mile block would thus be completed in 27 days. Allowing, as suggested at the beginning of the chapter for working about six days out of seven, this is equal to four and a half weeks. The lowest eight courses, 1470mm (58in), would be built in 54 days, or nine weeks. This, it must be remembered, is about the maximum height of surviving Broad Wall – and very little survives to that height.

A little more time has to be allowed to build up the wall at the ends of a gang length. To build an end four courses high takes ten stones on each side, with the core carefully built up as already described. A total of perhaps three extra days for each curtain might be allowed. This brings the total to five weeks for the first four courses, or ten weeks for the first eight courses.

The rate for laying the foundations was given above as 4m an hour. If this is rounded down to 30yds in an 8-hour day and 10 gangs were employed by each legion, then the foundation in a legionary length of 8100yds would be completed in 27 days, or less than five weeks, by 380 men.

In one legionary length there are 10 turrets. If one day is allowed for a gang to move from site to site, and two turret gangs were employed, totalling 96 men, then 25 days, or just over four weeks, would suffice to build all of a legion's turrets to a height of 1470mm (58in). There is a certain amount of work not included, such as monolithic threshold slabs for those turrets which had them, and a total of five weeks may be allowed.

If two milecastle gate-building gangs were employed, then at the rate given above they would complete the piers and arches for all five milecastles in 30 days or five weeks. This would involve 96 men.

The total thus allocated for milecastles, turrets and curtains is: curtain wall 1275, foundations 380, turrets 96, milecastles 96, total 1847 men. This leaves 553 men in each legion free for other work, such as any ground clearance needed, lime burning, transport, etc.

	Week 1 JULY	Week 2 JULY	Week 3 JULY	Week 4 JULY	Week 5 AUG	Week 6 AUG	Week 7 AUG	Week 8 AUG	Week 9 SEPT	Week 10 SEPT	Week 11 SEPT	Week 12 SEPT	Week 13 OCT	Week 14 OCT	Week 15 OCT
SO survey	■														
Preparatory orders			■												
Mensores aurvey					■										
Foundation quarrying						■	■	■							
Foundation build							■	■	■						
Turret quarrying/dressing						■	■	■	■						
Turret build – 8 courses									■	■					
MC gate quarrying/dressing							■	■	■						
MC gate build									■	■					
CW quarrying/dressing						■	■	■	■	■	■	■	■	■	
Curtain wall build – 4 courses / 8 courses									■	■	■	■	■	■	■

66 Chart showing a theoretical schedule of work for a legionary length

To summarise, within five weeks of beginning work a force of under 1900 men could build the curtain wall in a legionary length to a height of 735mm (29in), the turrets to a height of 1470mm (58in), and erect all the milecastle gate piers and arches. If building work began eight weeks after the initial decision, and quarrying began one week ahead of building work, then a total of 13 weeks would have elapsed. This is shown in the chart, *figure 66*, where the decision is shown as made on 1 July.

It is probable that work began while Hadrian was in the province. Working under the emperor's eye, the troops would have tended to be brisk and with at least the appearance of enthusiasm. Gangs spread out along the line of the Wall would have been an impressive sight, and the lowest first stages of the Wall could have been completed in a very short time. Even if 50 per cent were added to the times suggested, progress would still have been rapid. As has been discussed, building would have been in discrete sections. The figures given above indicate that while some sections would not have been started, others could have been built to a height of several feet within the time frame given. If Hadrian spent three or four months in Britain, there would have been ample time for him to have made the initial decision and to have revised the plans to include forts before he left.

The speed of building suggested above may seem inordinately quick. It must be remembered that building in squared rubble does not require a great degree of skill, and the men will have had at least some experience, and even more importantly, that those supervising will have fully understood the work in hand. Little or no time would have been wasted wondering how to set about it, and any problems encountered would not have been new ones. In the same way, working stone is *easy* once one has the experience, and achieving an accuracy of 1.5mm in 300mm (1/16in in a foot) is no more than average, and has been since the days of the Ancient Egyptians. Without substantial personal experience, trying to imagine oneself in the position of a individual carrying out any task is impossible.

It must be stressed yet again that the above is an intellectual exercise which gives an indication of how quickly the lower part of the Wall could have been built given a reasonably high level of organisation. It cannot be applied to the building of the whole Wall.

DITCH AND VALLUM

In view of the unique nature of the Vallum, it is worth taking a brief look at what labour input might have been necessary for the addition of this work to the Wall.

There are wide variations in the rates of excavation given in different sources. According to Rawlinson (Bruce 1851, 94), the nineteenth-century navvy could

'... remove the enormous quantity of twenty cubic yards of earth per day.' The length of the working day is not specified, but if of 10 effective hours, then the rate is just over one minute per cubic foot. Rawlinson's men were professional diggers of canals and railway cuttings, using iron shovels and wheelbarrows, and cannot fairly be compared with the legionaries who built the Wall.

Modern estimating tables for building work are not appropriate as most of this sort of work is now done by machine; older tables assume the use of the navvy, which the Roman soldier was not. The closest available parallel to the legionary is probably the early twentieth-century British soldier, a man who was basically fit and had had some practice in this sort of work. The Roman *dolabra* and spade, whether iron-shod or all iron, are not unlike the pick and shovel specified for the British field exercises. In the following discussion, British army figures will be used (War Office (1935), appendix XIV; War Office (1936), appendix II and III; War Office (1914), 98.).

For road cuttings up to 3m (10ft) deep the average output per man using a pick and shovel is reckoned at $0.5m^3$ (0.67 cu.yds) per hour in light clay (sand 1.36 cu.yds, hardpan 0.39 cu.yds). In the Great War, digging trenches, not under fire, British labour companies could dig to a depth of 1800mm (6ft) at the rate of $2.6m^3$ (90 cu.ft.) in 4 hours in stiff clay with flint or gravel requiring considerable pick work. Allowing 50 per cent extra time given in the tables for digging up to 3m (9ft) deep, this translates to a rate of $0.43m^3$ (0.55 cu.yds) an hour, or about $3.5m^2$ (4.5 cu.yds) in an 8-hour day.

If the British army figures are averaged, a rate of about $0.5m^3$ (0.6 cu.yds) an hour for digging the ditch and Vallum can be arrived at. This is just over one quarter of Rawlinson's rate for the navvy, but in his final calculations Rawlinson in fact allowed for use only of the 'ancient Briton ... driven to his ungrateful task' for whom he allows a rate of 8yds a day. This is still faster than suggested here for the Roman army, but the Roman soldier was no more a slave than he was a navvy; he was a trained soldier who occasionally dug ditches.

The cross-section of the 'typical' Vallum is $4.6m^2$ (5.55 sq.yds), and the length 112km (70 miles), giving a notional volume of material to be excavated of $1,465,313m^3$ (1,916,444 cu.yds). At the rate given above, this would have taken 1,577,550 man-hours, or 399,259 man-days.

Rather surprisingly, disposing of the spoil to either side into mounds would have taken somewhat longer than the excavation, if one assumes that the mounds were always revetted with turf. Moving soil on a stretcher is at the rate of two man-minutes per cubic foot. If movement were in baskets, the same rate would apply as one man could not move loads of 1 cu.ft of soil at a time all day. Excavated material, taking an average between loam and clay, weighs about 1450kg per cubic metre (90lb per cubic foot). Shovelling the excavated earth into baskets is at twice this rate, averaged over 8 hours. Digging turf and building a revetment is at the rate of 3m² (32 sq.ft) per hour. Loading, moving and dumping and revetting comes to 550,407 man-days. The total thus arrived at for excavating the ditch and building the mounds is 949,667 man-days.

On the same terms, and on the calculation that it was 95km (59 miles) long, the Wall ditch amounted to 1,071,846m³ (1,401,840 cu.yds) and would have taken 292,050 man-days to excavate. Spreading the upcast carefully into a smooth glacis is at the rate given above for filling baskets, that is 35 man-minutes per cubic metre (one man-minute per cubic foot). This amounts to 78,854 man-days, with a total for excavation and the glacis of 370,904 man-days.

Inscriptions from the Vallum are too few in number to estimate how many men might have been engaged on its excavation at any one time. As an example, and no more, six *cohortes quingenariae peditatae* might yield a work force of around 1800. These men could dig the Vallum and raise the mounds in 527 days, or about two and a half seasons. The same number working on the ditch would complete it in 206 days, or about one season.

These figures make no allowance for digging through rock, which would have taken longer than the time saved when digging through easy soil, nor is any allowance made for the weight of excavated rock rather than soil, nor for incomplete digging of the ditch, nor incomplete smoothing of the glacis. However, the calculations give an indication of the relative scale of the works.

One major problem in any calculations is that in modern times all-steel shovel blades are available, whereas it was normal in Roman times for shovels to be of wood tipped with an iron edge. These would be less efficient owing to the increased thickness of the edge and greater friction of the blade. It must be emphasised that the figures do not purport to show how long the Vallum or ditch actually took to dig: they provide no more than an indication of the scale of the works relative to each other and to the overall work of building the Wall complex.

STANDARDS OF WORKMANSHIP

The curtain wall is of roughly squared coursed rubble, and as such the individual stones are of adequate quality. It could be argued that with more attention paid to squaring the stones the appearance would have been better, but the author is unable to see any change in the standard from the start of the Broad Wall to the completion of the Narrow Wall. The Romans built what they were intending to build, and what was built is recognisably satisfactory.

The worked stone, that is principally the gate piers, is a different matter. There are wide variations in the surface finish: the flat, chiselled face on the north-east pier of MC10; the flat, carefully pecked faces of Benwell Vallum Crossing; the stones which are little more than large squared rubble at MC48; the shallow, punched rock faces at MC37; the poorly worked stones of both gates of MC42; and the more or less flat faces of the east gate at Birdoswald. Those stones which have a rock face are defined by chiselled margins, but these are very often ill-worked and rounded, and in many cases not completed. The rock faces even within one pier can vary widely in their projection and finish.

Those faces clearly intended to be worked to a straight-edge rarely achieve the intention. Even the western stone of the north-east pier of MC10, definitely one of the better ones, is straight over only two thirds of the face. The general impression given by most gateways is that near enough was good enough.

The standard of training needed to produce the piers of the fort and milecastle gateways is considerably higher than that required for the curtain wall, but in such a major project every man who showed the slightest aptitude seems to have been called upon to work above the level of his training. The gate piers are structurally adequate but the quality of workmanship shown on the faces is generally mediocre. Standing out from the others is Benwell Vallum Crossing. Here was a gateway built with real skill and effort, a piece of high-quality, though not fault-free, work carried out by skilled men, which points up the distinction between the average poorly trained soldier and the legionary stonemason.

Practical trials with samples of stones from quarries along the line of the Wall show that, in some cases at least, it would have been perfectly possible to produce higher quality work with little effort if some investment in training had been made. If the army, or the emperor, had accepted a delay of perhaps six months before starting construction, and a longer delay in completing the work, it would have been a relatively simply matter to train large numbers of legionaries to a far higher standard than was evidently available. In the event, this was regarded as unimportant, hence the ill-worked, half-finished stones which are typical of milecastle and fort gateways on the Wall. Perhaps even more relevant than the level of training is the obvious lack of care about the appearance of the finished work. The standards of workmanship are discussed further in the next chapter.

10

DISLOCATION

It has long been accepted that at some point in the programme the building of the curtain wall, milecastles, and turrets was disrupted or halted for an indeterminate time, when work began on the addition of forts to the line of the Wall itself. This event is usually referred to as 'dislocation'.

At about the same time as dislocation, a decision was made to reduce the gauge of the curtain wall from 10Rf to about 8Rf or even less – the change from Broad Wall to Narrow Wall, which is one of the factors which enables the point of dislocation to be identified.

PROGRESS AT DISLOCATION

To determine progress at the point of dislocation is not easy. Many older reports do not clearly distinguish between the body of the Wall and the footing courses, or between footings and foundations. Much early work concentrated on the location of structures, and sections across the curtain wall or milecastle walls were sometimes recorded just as 'Broad Wall' or 'Narrow Wall.'

The identification of structures begun in Broad Wall but completed in Narrow Wall is not always straightforward, but two rules have been followed. First, where the curtain wall or any wall of a milecastle is less than 8.9Rf (8ft 6in/2590mm) wide, the structure is here regarded as completed in Narrow Wall. It is true that narrow side walls to milecastles occur in association with Broad north walls. But this is precisely what is to be expected, as the (broad) north walls seem to have been built first. It cannot be assumed that any structure *begun* in Broad Wall was inevitably *completed* to that gauge. To put it simply, if a gang had competed only a few courses when the order came to reduce the gauge, they are most unlikely to complete their work to the top in Broad gauge on the grounds that that is how they started.

Secondly, where Broad Wall is recorded at a structure but the only record of curtain wall to one side or both sides is of Narrow Wall, the structure is again seen as completed in Narrow Wall. This follows the argument put forward above that no structure would have been taken above the first 1200-1500mm (4-5ft) in height until scaffolding was available as part of the progress of the curtain wall.

Broad foundation is regarded as a minimum of 9.9Rf. This is to some extent arbitrary, but the selected figure has some justification. The limit of 9.9Rf for the broad foundation is well below what ought to be the foundation for a wall of 10Rf, but it takes into account the abandoned broad foundation east of MC39 which is 9.95Rf. The Wall was designed to be 10Rf wide and, while some deviation is inevitable in squared rubble construction, a reduction of a full Roman foot is a significant amount. It is, of course, possible that some gangs managed to build the Wall well below specifications.

The following summaries mention in detail only those sites where the situation merits explanation.

13.2.1 WALLSEND TO MC4

All the curtain wall appears to have been Narrow. What appears to be Broad foundation has been found near St Francis Community Centre, close to T0b, but this has been interpreted as Narrow foundation which has widened due to movement and fissures. Nothing relevant is known of the milecastles and turrets.

13.2.2 MC4 TO NORTH TYNE

The milecastles
From and including MC4 to MC27 there are 24 milecastles. Some evidence is available for 15 of them: MCs 4, 9, 10, 13, 14, 17, 18, 19, 20, 22, 23, 24, 25, 26, and 27. Of these, eight have at least some narrow side or south walls: MCs 4, 9, 13, 17, 18, 19, 20, 22. MC4 is taken as a Narrow Wall milecastle as it seems to the author that the superstructure of the fragment of side wall must have been in the region of 9Rf wide. The fact that MC18 has a type I north gate set in a broad north wall and yet is long axis suggests that it was begun by legion A and completed by another post-dislocation. MC22 has a broad north wall, with Broad Wall immediately to the west, but narrow side walls (8.24Rf) which had no broad foundation. The other seven milecastles, MCs 10, 14, 23, 24, 25, 26, 27, are known to have had

broad side walls, at least at the very low level to which they survived. As very few milecastles have been fully excavated it is possible that the list of milecastles completed after dislocation could be extended.

Turrets

In this length of Wall there were 46 turrets; information is available on six, Ts7b, 19a, 19b, 25b, 26a, and 26b. Three of these, turrets 7b, 19a, and 19b, have Broad Wall known close to or abutting their wing walls and at intervals between them. This might suggest that all three were finished before dislocation, but the picture is not straightforward. There is Broad Wall close to MCs 19 and 20, meeting the east wing wall in the case of the latter, yet they were both completed with narrow gauge side walls. At T26a it is not certain that the broad foundation was completed below the east wing wall before the decision to narrow the curtain wall. Turret 26b has broad wing walls, met by Narrow Wall on the east side and by Broad Wall on the west side. As the eastern wing wall is no more than a metre in height, completion of the turret must relate to the later phase of work.

Curtain wall

Looking at the 70 intervals between structures from MC4 to North Tyne, useful information on the curtain wall is recorded in 23 of them. Of these, only eight provide evidence at more than one point in the interval. In most monuments this would not be a problem; it would be eminently reasonable to assume a constant width. On Hadrian's Wall, where the gauge is known to have changed, this assumption cannot be made. Looking at the intervals rather than the number of individual references, twenty show Broad Wall and eight show Narrow Wall; the numbers do not tally as three intervals show both broad and narrow.

This should not be seen as a statistical analysis: there are too many intervals where there has been no excavation. Only in the curtain wall from MC19 to T19b can there be any degree of certainty that Broad Wall exists throughout, and even there, as the milecastles at each side were finished to narrow gauge, there can be no certainty that the curtain wall was completed to full height as designed. It would be more accurate to say that from MC19 to T19b all the curtain wall may have been *begun* in broad gauge.

Broad foundation

Almost every record from just east of T7b to North Tyne shows broad foundation beneath the curtain wall; the only small question mark comes from T26a as discussed above. The likelihood is that broad foundation for the curtain wall was laid throughout this length, although not under all the milecastles.

NORTH TYNE TO THE RIVER IRTHING

Milecastles

Of the 21 milecastles in this sector useful information is available on 11. Of these, seven were begun in Broad Wall; five of these, MCS 35, 37, 38, 41, 42, were completed in Narrow Wall. Two of them, MCS 47 and 48, *may* have been completed to broad specification but this is seen as unlikely as there is no Broad Wall known in their vicinity. Four milecastles, 33, 36, 39, 40, were built wholly in Narrow Wall.

A raking joint in the north wall of MC33, which has narrow walls, may indicate that the piers had been built and a small start made on the north face of a broad north wall when dislocation occurred. MC35 may have been begun in broad gauge; the small section of apparent Broad Wall at the south-west corner may be an indication of this, but the amount of rebuilding carried out there makes certainty impossible.

MC37 has a tapered north wall, clearly showing that it was completed post-dislocation, and the side walls are on the defined borderline between Broad and Narrow.

The north wall of MC40 has broad foundation beneath the east wing wall, with one course inset by 175mm (7in) and a second course inset above that, but all four walls are narrow. It may be that the building of the milecastle had only just begun when work was dislocated but there is no certainty.

Little is known of MC43. The fragmentary remains of the side walls are measured from the excavator's drawing as 2590mm (8ft 6in) wide, but there does not appear to be evidence to support this width as only one edge of each of the side walls was found. Although only the southern edge of the foundation beneath the north wall was seen, it may be reasonably assumed as broad in view of the broad foundation found immediately to the west of Greatchesters.

Turrets

There were 44 turrets in this length of the Wall, of which relevant information is available for 14. Half of these were begun in Broad Wall, the remainder in Narrow Wall.

Turret 33b has broad but low wing walls, and T34a has broad but low and very short wing walls indicating that at both sites work had only just been started at the change of gauge. No measurements are available for T36b, but as it underlies Housesteads fort it ought to have been started in Broad Wall. Turret 41a has a broad north wall but the wing walls were never built (see below, *Broad foundation*); it looks as though work had just begun on the turret. Turret 43a is built on the broad foundation and was almost certainly begun before dislocation (see below, *Broad foundation*). Turret 45a, a pre-Wall tower or very early turret, has no broad foundation, although the foundation close to either side is as much as 355mm (14in) wider than the Narrow Wall adjacent to the turret.

It is most unlikely that any of the turrets examined in this sector were completed before the change in gauge of the Wall.

Curtain wall

There are two small lengths of Broad Wall: one abuts Willowford Bridge; the other occurs about 100m east of T48b, where there are traces remaining of Broad Wall superstructure which amount to a few stones on top of broad footings. Clearly, a gang was beginning work on building Broad Wall onto the extensive broad footings in this area. In the rest of this sector, there is only one piece of curtain wall, other than a wing wall, which is not narrow gauge. This is on the west side of T48b, where the curtain wall tapers down from the turret to a point 13m (39ft) to the west at which point is was 2310mm (7ft 7in/7.8Rf).

Broad foundation

Turret T29b has uncompleted broad foundation on the east side represented by two marginal stones at the southern edge with nothing inside them.

Immediately to the west of Housesteads fort the excavator believed that the broad foundation had been started but not completed before the gauge of the Wall was reduced. From Highshield Crags westwards there are short stretches of broad foundation, some of which were ignored by the builders of the Narrow Wall who laid new narrow foundation. The north-east corner of MC39 also has a small length of broad foundation beneath the curtain wall.

About 100yds east of T41a there is a short stretch of what appears to be broad foundation (with no footing course) which quickly tapers back to the narrow foundation. Below where the wing walls at T41a would have been, the only visible remnant is a single line of stones as an edge to the broad foundation, which had no corework and was clearly unfinished.

From the west side of Greatchesters fort, unused broad foundations run on a line separate from the later narrow foundation to the site of T43a which sits on the broad foundation; the two gauges then separate again to beyond Cockmount Hill. The fact that the Narrow Wall converged with broad foundation at the turret suggests that the turret had been partly built at the point of dislocation, and was thus begun in Broad Wall. The broad foundation is strictly foundation only and includes no footing course. A small length of the narrow foundation either side of T45a is on a slightly different alignment from the Narrow Wall superstructure, but the relevance of this is uncertain.

West of T48b the gauge tapers as described above (and the excavator's drawing shows clearly that the foundation as well as the Wall is tapered), although at about the same point broad foundation has been found more recently (Shaw 1926; Whitworth 1997).

Broad foundation was clearly very much unfinished in this sector.

DISLOCATION – DISCUSSION

It seems clear that the Broad Wall was by no means finished to the east of North Tyne before work began to the west. Not only were there stretches of broad curtain wall not built, but eight out of the fifteen known milecastles were completed in narrow gauge. One of the six known turrets was certainly not completed, and completion of the remainder cannot be assured. Probably all the broad foundation beneath the curtain wall was laid.

The curtain wall at Planetrees is significant in that it shows the only confirmed point of reduction other than at a turret, and it holds lessons for other observations. It would be remarkable if this were the only point at which the gauge was changed between structures, and records of 'Broad Wall' cannot be held to be constant throughout an interval between structures unless examination has been made at a large number of points. If century lengths were really as short as 6m (20ft) and cohort lengths 36m (120ft) then, especially in areas where Broad and Narrow Wall are known to exist, examination at intervals of no more than, say, 50m (150ft) is necessary to establish a full record of the width as actually built.

Furthermore, the same caveat must be applied to horizontal changes to the curtain wall. A few surviving courses of Broad Wall do not mean, given the way in which any type of wall is built, that it was so completed. The vertical offset at Planetrees, the only remaining sign of a junction between Broad and Narrow wall, west of MC26, shows how the change from Broad to Narrow was effected at the end of a gang length which had been started in broad, but no evidence remains of how the change was effected in the horizontal plane. It is most unlikely that a partly built gang length would be completed to the top in Broad Wall after the change in gauge had been made. The way in which Narrow Wall rides over the broad wing walls suggests that a single wide offset would have been used, but it could also have been done by a succession of small offsets (67).

The probably way in which the reduction at Planetrees would have been effected is shown in *figure 68*. Whichever method was used, once fallen the remains would be unlikely to show any evidence for an offset.

It is important to re-emphasise that the Wall was built in a series of discrete sections and in a number of horizontal stages. Uniformity is not to be expected in a wall which did not unroll over the countryside as a 15ft entity.

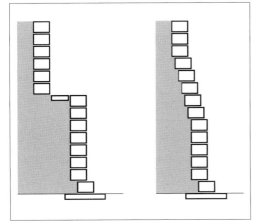

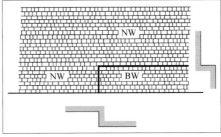

Left: 67 Two ways of reducing the width of the curtain wall

Above: 68 The probable appearance at Planetrees on completion

Evidence from excavations shows that, while the north walls, and perhaps the south gates, of the milecastles might be started, the side walls might be left until later, a point discussed in some detail by Hunneysett, 1980. The fact that a part of a structure was built in Broad Wall does not necessarily mean that it was completed before the change of gauge occurred. It is clear from the excavations of MC22 that broad foundation was not always laid under the side walls of milecastles with broad north walls until work began on their completion. To that limited extent broad foundation was not laid throughout the eastern sector. The picture of construction work which emerges is very much as one would expect. There were clearly many gangs of men at work simultaneously throughout Hooley and Breeze's four legionary lengths from just east of MC7 to the North Tyne, and they had not finished when dislocation occurred. The hard evidence for *completion* of a structure to broad gauge is no greater at, say, MC27, than at MC10.

There were clearly many gangs at work between North Tyne and the Irthing as well, putting in broad foundations and beginning to build in Broad Wall before the sector east of North Tyne was complete. Progress was apparently not so far advanced; seven of the known milecastles were begun in Broad Wall but, at most, only two may have been so completed. Four were not begun until the change in gauge. Half of the 14 known turrets were begun in broad gauge, although probably none of them was completed before the gauge was reduced. Much of the broad foundation was incomplete, although too few intervals (38 out of 65) provide information on which to base an estimate of the percentages. Only fragments of broad curtain wall are known to have been started.

East of North Tyne 53 per cent of known milecastles and 16 per cent of the known turrets were completed to the narrow gauge, compared with 82 per cent and 50 per cent respectively west of North Tyne. It must be emphasised once again that the samples are small and almost certainly do not present an accurate picture.

Although work is believed to have been divided into legionary blocks which were equal to one season's work (Hooley and Breeze 1968; Breeze and Dobson 2000, 75-6), the evidence indicates very clearly that no one block was completed before the next one was started. Breeze and Dobson show legion B at work in sectors 7-12 and 22-27a, legion A in 12-17 and 36b-43, and legion C in 17-22 and 43-49. As none of these sectors was completed in broad gauge and yet there is Broad Wall represented in every single legionary length (in structures if not in curtain wall), all three legions must have been divided along the whole length of their several sectors from the beginning. It is probable that there were gangs working on curtain wall, turrets, and milecastles simultaneously, although the proportion of men allocated to each probably varied from legion to legion (Hunneysett 1980, 102).

What is less clear is the length of time which may have elapsed between the start east of North Tyne and the start to the west. It has been argued that a building gang of 30 could build 18m (20yds) of Wall to a height of 735mm (29in) in one day. The model allows for all the curtain wall in a legionary length to be built up to four courses high in five weeks. However, as has been shown, not all the Broad Wall was even begun in the eastern sector.

There are 30 distinct records of broad curtain wall, that is excluding turrets, milecastles, and their wing walls, between T7b and North Tyne. If each of 15 gangs built two recorded instances of Broad Wall, the amount of *known* broad curtain wall, as opposed to foundation and footings, in this sector could have been completed in a week or so. There is no *evidence* for more than about four weeks' work from Newcastle to the North Tyne including milecastles and turrets. Hunneysett points out that the legion working immediately east of MC22 (close to Dere Street) was concentrating on completion of curtain wall, and that to the west was concentrating on milecastles. As these legions were thus doing only a part of the work allocated to them, the time needed to complete the amount of Broad Wall known to have been built is reduced.

The suggested rate of work is of course theoretical, and the difference in overall working time east and west of North Tyne is not easy to quantify. Given that the topography of the crags makes for more difficult transport and working conditions, there need not have been any great interval between starting work in the east and starting in the west.

The records suggest that a start had been made on the MC4–North Tyne sector, perhaps to impress the emperor (Corbridge would have been an ideal place for him to stay). Some gangs were then moved to the central sector as it was convenient to begin work there. This movement would have involved delay and reorganisation, and it might have been no more than another month or so before plans were revised and the decision made to put forts on to the line of the Wall and to dig the Vallum. As has been suggested, this could all have been done during Hadrian's visit to the province.

It could be that the two sectors were begun at the same time, but with a much greater number of men allocated to the eastern sector. This model has the advantage of explaining the considerable progress with MCs 47 and 48, and the start of Ts48a and b as possibly early design turrets with broad wing walls and a narrow north wall.

In fact, in the present state of knowledge, the best that can be said is that the evidence so far points to greater progress to the east than to the west of North Tyne, but that east of North Tyne a considerable amount of work was uncompleted before the change of gauge.

However, only limited weight can be put on the perceived completion ratio between Narrow Wall and Broad Wall. Fewer than one third of the structures excavated have yielded relevant information, and the sampling has not been done on any formal basis. Even the information to hand is by no means complete, as a number of excavations were limited to answering certain specific questions such as the type of gateway, the width of turret walls, or the position of the doorway. Unless it is possible to excavate a turret to beyond the normal length of the wing walls, and the wing walls and turret are found to be standing at least several courses high, any possible evidence for Narrow Wall would be missing. More turrets in the east may have been finished in Narrow Wall than have so far been identified from the very small sample. Equally, it is possible that more turrets and milecastles in the central sector than are now known were begun in Broad Wall.

THE NARROW WALL DECISION

That the effect of this decision impinged on the structures and the curtain wall is clear: the width of the Wall is reduced from 10Rf to as little as 6Rf. Milecastle walls were reduced in thickness, and those turrets not yet started had narrow wing walls. What is less clear is the relationship of this decision to the fort decision. The Narrow Wall may have preceded the fort decision or they may have been coincident; the Narrow Wall decision cannot have come significantly later than the fort decision as no fort, so far as is known, is abutted by the superstructure of the Broad Wall.

On the west side of Chesters, the fort ditch had been dug before the broad foundation, which overlies the infilled end of the ditch, indicating that the Narrow Wall decision came after the fort decision, although by how long is not discernible. At Housesteads, it seems that by the time the fort ditches were dug the decision had been made to reduce the thickness of the Wall. It is not possible to say at what point in the construction of a fort ditches were dug; logically they ought to have come after the completion of the fort walls to allow easy access for men and materials, but at all three forts they do seem to have come very early.

The fort ditches on the west side of Greatchesters were cut to stop just short of the broad foundation, the builders presumably believing that it was the Broad Wall which was to be built.

One would expect there to have been wing walls to the forts for bonding with the curtain wall, just as at milecastles and turrets; they certainly appear at Balmuildy on the Antonine Wall. These do not appear on the Wall forts, and it is significant that at Housesteads, and probably at Chesters, the Wall is not bonded with the fort wall. This could indicate that it was realised that it would be some time before the curtain wall would arrive. On the other hand, the builders of the fort may simply have made life easy for themselves by not providing wing walls. The Narrow Wall is bonded with Greatchesters fort, albeit in a rather strange way. The fort appears to have been completed after AD 128 and it may be that here the Narrow Wall was being built at the same time as the fort.

There is some evidence from milecastles. At MC37 there is a very small amount of Broad Wall to each side of the north gate; the tapered Narrow Wall leads off from these small triangles with an offset of up to 50mm (2in). It has long been known that work on MC37 was affected by dislocation, and it has been argued that the north gate piers were incomplete at this time. It appears that the piers and arches were completed after resumption of work following dislocation, after which a start was made on the north wall to the broad gauge. There would be no need at all to build any of the north wall until the piers had been built up to the capitals (it would in fact have been in the way). This suggests, and nothing more, that the Narrow Wall decision was not implemented until after the fort decision, although the interval need not have been long.

The interval between work on the Wall being temporarily abandoned in favour of the forts, or for other reasons, could have been a very short one, or it could have been long. Crow (1991) points out that at Peel Gap there must have been a considerable interval between the laying of the foundation and the building of the Narrow Wall. This is not to say, however, that this situation occurrred at all points. It has long been held that at least one legion was left at work in the central sector completing the work of others (e.g. Breeze and Dobson 2000), as there are inscriptions naming Nepos from MCs 37, 38, and 42, and work may have proceeded at once in some places and more slowly in others. However, given the possible speed of building suggested, the interval could have been up to, say, two years, and still fallen within the governorship of Nepos.

THE VALLUM DECISION

The Vallum seems to be approximately co-incident with the fort decision. There is a somewhat irregular diversion around Benwell which has been suggested as indicating that the fort was under construction. The western half is very regular, with one large and one small change in orientation. It should not have been difficult to repeat this on the eastern side, as indicated on *figure 69*, but instead it has a more sinuous appearance although set out in a series of straight lines.

At Rudchester there is some indication that on the west side the Vallum was being dug before the fort was planned (Bowden and Blood 1991). On the other hand, the ditch diggers may simply have forgotten that a fort was to be allowed for. At Greatchesters, the gap left in the Vallum indicates that the fort was already planned when the Vallum was dug in this area, even if no building work had begun.

From such evidence as there is, it is not impossible that the Vallum decision was made after the fort decision, but the question must remain open. Any interval may have been very short.

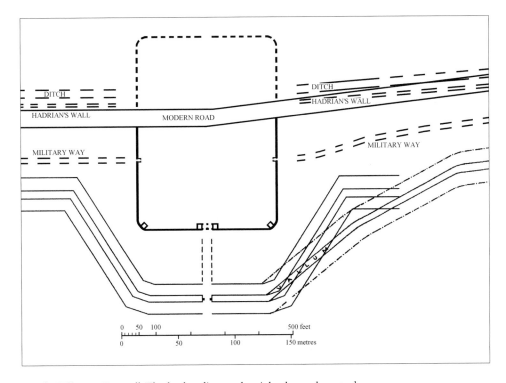

69 The Vallum at Benwell. The broken line to the right shows the actual course

A SECOND DISLOCATION?

The impression given by very many parts of the Wall is strongly that of a job where the nature of the supervision changed markedly. At first, is seems that the men carrying out the work, some of whom were skilled and some much less so, were supervised with an insistence on work of at least adequate quality. This was followed, post-dislocation, by a relaxing of standards. The changes are not immediately obvious, but they are there.

There then appears to have been a second 'dislocation' in work on the Wall. There was clearly a second dislocation at Birdoswald, demonstrated archaeologically as well as by masonry survey.[1] It was after the second break in construction there that the quality dropped markedly. The south-west pier of the west gate was begun well (there are only two stones remaining), and it sits on a well worked foundation block. Beneath the *spina* of this gate the western foundation block is similar but the block to the east, carrying the gate pivot, is a very poor stone which is little better than a natural boulder (*70*). The *spina* itself is very poorly worked. At the *porta quintana dextra* the north-east pier was begun reasonably well (there is now only one stone remaining), but the upper part of the south-east pier is little more than roughed-out.

70 The *spina* foundation, south side, Birdoswald west gate

There is good evidence from other forts. At Chesters, the north gate seems to have been started with a great deal of skill shown; at the east gate, the south-west pier is worked to a reasonable standard and shows ample skill and care taken with the cap. But the base of the south-east pier of this gate is clearly unfinished (*71*), with only the bottom part of the internal return completed.

The foundations of the north gate at Housesteads are of high quality beneath the north-east and north *spina* piers; the foundations beneath the north-west pier are markedly less well worked, something which is not directly relevant to their different design. At the west gate, the south-west pier was not well worked. The north-west pier is good at the base, but the top two courses show marked deterioration as though time was of the essence. The west pier of the *spina* at this gate shows a remarkable lack of care, and the topmost stone, which contains the locking bar hole, is frankly dreadful.

The same effect is to be seen on the north gateway of MC37. The lower courses of the piers are what might be described as honest Roman military engineering, but the upper part is noticeably worse; the cap of the south-east pier is particularly badly worked and the caps of the northern piers are not only bad but unfinished (*72*).

71 The south-east pier, Chesters east gate

72 The cap on the north-west pier, MC37 north gate

73 The north-west pier, MC42 south gate

The piers of MC42 are of bold appearance, but when examined individually and in close detail are far from well worked, showing a fairly consistent lack of care and skill. This is especially evident on the north-west pier, where the north face is little more than unworked, rough stone which was not dressed back to any sort of face (73). Again, this is a stone which was never finished. The north gate is no better than the south, although much less masonry remains. At MC10, the base of the north-east pier shows remarkably high quality on the face, while the west pier is much worse. The poor work in the piers of Broad Wall MC48, Poltross Burn, can be entirely explained by the very difficult nature of the stone used there.

It is probably true that some skill was lacking but, although the poor quality of some of the later work at Birdoswald, Housesteads, MC42, MC37, and MC10, may be in part due to a skills shortage, the overwhelming impression is that the philosophy behind the work had changed. Instead of a desire to produce work of good and impressive appearance, albeit lacking in sophistication and careful finish, there seems to have been a strong element of carelessness and 'near enough is good enough' creeping in.

There was then another change, marked by the fixing of unfinished stones. Now, instead of a lackadaisical approach, there seems to have been an urge to get the work finished regardless of whether the stones had been fully worked or not. The distinction is important. The differences between the upper and lower parts of the west gate at Housesteads, and between the upper and lower parts of the piers of MC37, are there, and when the stones are subjected to detailed examination they can be demonstrated, but they are not always immediately apparent, especially to the non-specialist.

No demonstration is needed as to the condition of the pier caps at MC37, the lowest stone of the south-east pier of Chesters east gate, the north-west pier of the south gate at MC42, the south pier of the *porta decumana dextra* at Birdoswald, the west gate *spina* foundation at the same fort, or the upper *spina* at Housesteads. These stones are not badly finished, they are simply unfinished.

It is not the case that they were being worked *in situ* when some other task supervened. The pier stone at Chesters east gate is worked from the bottom bed, which cannot have been done after fixing. Similarly the cap of the north-west pier at MC37 was worked from the underside. In both cases the work done on the stones was carried out before they were fixed in position. It seems to have become a matter of completing the work as fast as possible without the slightest regard for the appearance.

To summarise, when work began on the gateways of both milecastles and forts there was a philosophy of making a good, sound job of work within the limitations of the skills available. Then, when work had been underway for a comparatively short time, standards were lowered; there was greater stress placed on getting the work completed. Again after short time, there was a major change with considerable pressure to complete the work in any fashion.

If the chronology for the making of the fort decision suggested above is accepted, it is not impossible that the departure of the emperor and the first dislocation may have led to the initial relaxation in quality.

The reason for the second, and very visible change is less easy to understand. Stevens (1966) suggested that there may have been fighting during the building; others have argued against the idea of any fighting in Britain during Hadrian's reign after AD 119 (e.g. Jarrett 1976). Casey (1987), on the other hand, suggests that there was fighting in the middle 120s. It is not within the compass of this book to examine whether or not there was fighting, but such an event would explain much. If the legions, after beginning work on the forts, were taken off the building work to spend one or more seasons fighting, they could well have been reluctant to return to work on a wall 80 miles long. They may have rebelled against the additional work and been allowed to complete the work to their own standards. The second dislocation may (there is no evidence) have been the result of a major halt in building, with work continuing at different times in the forts and the milecastles. This hypothesis would help to accommodate the situation at Birdoswald, where it would hardly be possible to fit in the start of a turf and timber fort, replacement by a stone fort, and two dislocations, before the end of the governorship of Nepos. The fact that some milecastle gateways were completed in that time does not necessarily mean that the forts were completed at the same time.

It is also possible that the extra work, and perhaps the attitude of the legions, led to auxiliaries being drafted in to assist, not in their own right with their own inscriptions, but as additional labour for the legions. Their comparative lack of experience in stone building may have led to a lowering of standards.

Neither explanation finds much favour with the author. Their chief merit is that they would fit the few known facts.

11

SUMMARY

This study has examined the methods, techniques, and operations necessary for the building of Hadrian's Wall. The examination has taken a different approach from previous work in that it is based on the application of personal, practical experience of masonry work. This has resulted in a picture of the Wall which is rather different from the received view, and some aspects of the building process have taken on greater significance than was previously thought to be the case.

The conventional view of the Wall is that it was begun, or at least planned, during the visit of the emperor in 122. After some one or two seasons' work, during which the Wall was virtually completed as planned between Newcastle and the River North Tyne, major changes were made. Forts were built as an integral part of the Wall and the Vallum dug as a line of demarcation to the south, and at about the same time the thickness of the Wall was reduced. These changes caused a dislocation of the building gangs, which may have led one legion to continue work started by another. The work is generally seen as being of high quality.

The view taken here is rather different. The appearance of the Wall, massive and imposing, will have dominated the landscape in a way not seen in any other frontier, yet it is a work of often inferior quality when examined in detail. The workmanship along the Wall varies markedly from excellent to very poor indeed. The Wall will have been impressive from a distance, much less so from close up. If the emperor had delayed the start of work for six months, a great many men could have been trained to a significantly higher standard. Hadrian, or perhaps the army, was not concerned with a work of high quality, but rather a work of unprecedented and impressive scale. Other Hadrianic work in Britain is of far higher quality; for example, there is nothing on the Wall which can compare with the Hadrianic inscription from Wroxeter, *RIB* 288. The Wall is for the most part a utilitarian work of military engineering carried out by the army to low but acceptable standards. It has been argued from an examination of the evidence that the curtain wall was not rendered. It is not impossible that the curtain wall was limewashed, although the evidence is at present lacking.

The comparatively high quality of some parts shows that the legions were capable of much better work than is generally seen on the Wall. The fact that there was large-scale rebuilding under Severus only 80 years later indicates that the curtain wall was in a state of collapse, probably as a result of being built hastily under pressure to complete as quickly as possible. It seems to have been built for imperial effect rather than for the utility of its design, something emphasised by the later abandonment of turrets and the blocking of many milecastle gateways.

The possible rate of building put forward, allied to the simple nature of the surveying needed, suggests that at least the initial work on the Wall may well have been much quicker than has previously been put forward. This makes existing timetables for the work uncertain, although not enough is known about the Wall to attempt a programme for the whole of the work.

The widespread, although not uniform, occurrence of Broad Wall in all legionary lengths between Newcastle and the River Irthing indicates that small gangs were at work simultaneously at very many points. Alongside this, the argument that there is no evidence for completion of any part of the Wall to the original Broad gauge makes it possible for both the initial decision and the changes in plan to have occurred during Hadrian's time in the province.

There is good evidence that there was a second dislocation of work as shown by a second, very marked, drop in quality of work in the fort and milecastle gateways along with the fixing of clearly unfinished stones. This may have been no more than a sudden, unexplained, change in philosophy; alternatively it may have been the result of fighting in the province leading to disaffection among the legions.

There is a long-held and widely accepted view that the stone was normally 'very carefully selected'; the evidence put forward here suggests that stone was taken from a large number of small quarries all along the line of the Wall and was chosen chiefly for its location rather than its quality. The greatest distance from quarry to Wall is probably just over 1 mile, from Black Pasture to Chesters fort. The manifestly inferior stone used for the gateways of MC48 came from the valley of the Poltross Burn, some 50yds away.

The use of these many small quarries will have had a serious impact on the local environment. The constant passage of pack animals and carts criss-crossing the whole area must have made the use of existing arable fields next to impossible; grazing will also have been affected. This, added to the use of cultivated fields for the line of the Wall itself, must have given rise to considerable disaffection and may have given impetus to any fighting occurring during the building programme.

It has been argued that scaffolding was not only essential but that the enormous quantities needed would have put a considerable strain on local resources and may have been a limiting factor on the rate of building the upper parts of the Wall. This adds weight to the limit on the amount of work completed before dislocation.

The examination of the transport requirements in relation to what had to be transported has argued that the Roman army had wagons available which could readily cope with payloads of 2 tons. Carts and smaller wagons could probably have carried greater loads than hitherto thought likely. The review of pack transport argues that, given the short journeys from quarry to site, pack animals could carry four typical walling stones.

Milecastles are unique in size and form; no other Hadrianic fortlets approaching this size have two gateways and a roadway running through. In addition, the manning level, 8-12 men in 'standard' milecastles, is much lower than for any other fortlet, apart perhaps from signal stations. Fortlets of similar morphology were included in the design of the Antonine Wall, but were somewhat larger. The form was not repeated elsewhere in the empire; even the *Fossatum Africae* has gateways of the Knag Burn type rather than milecastles. The detailed description of the building of milecastle walls has led to an understanding of why the external corners are rounded: it is simpler to build round corners than square ones when using roughly squared rubble, and thus more appropriate for men with limited skills.

An estimate has been made of the possible labour force, and this suggests that a century had perhaps only 50 men available for construction work, with a total legionary labour force in the order of 7200.

One point which has emerged during this study is that comparatively little is known about the Wall in detail. Excavations of a limited number of sites have perforce been used to provide a view of the Wall as a whole. From Wallsend to the Irthing there were 49 milecastles of which information is available on only 27. In some cases the amount of information is very small; for example, all that is known of MCS 23-26 is that the side walls were 'Broad'.

These pages cannot be the last word on the building of the Wall. It is hoped that they will inspire others to take a detailed interest in the way it was built and to refine the conclusions reached here.

ENDNOTES

CHAPTER 1

1 Tacitus (*Agricola* XXIII) says that Agricola established *praesidia* (garrisons) across the Forth-Clyde isthmus.

CHAPTER 3

1 This is the pattern of two sets of heavily incised grooves crossing diagonally on the face of the stone. A broach is a northern or Scottish term for a punch, and broaching is a similarly derived term for work done with punch.
2 Note, this is the correct form of the word often written as template; see *OED* etc.

CHAPTER 6

1 The figures assume that initially only forts to the east of the River Irthing were to be in stone and excludes Carvoran and the later fort at Carrawburgh. All had four double-portal gates and two single-portal *portae quintanae* gates, except Wallsend (one single-portal gate) and Housesteads and Greatchesters without *portae quintanae*. MCS 0 and 43 were replaced by forts.

CHAPTER 7

1 The author is grateful to Sergeant Major Kohler, Defence Animal Centre, Melton Mowbray, in charge (2001) of Army pack transport training, and to Major R. Hill (retired) who was in charge of training 2500 pack ponies in Scotland for a projected invasion of Norway in 1942.

CHAPTER 9

1 Tacitus implies that after the rebellion of Boudica the legions were kept in tents outside the normal campaigning season; the fact that he mentions this suggests that it was an unusual occurrence (*Annals* XIV, 28).

2 Tacitus has Calgacus complain that 'Our limbs and bodies are worn out in clearing woods and draining marshes ...' (*Agricola* XXXI) implying the use of forced labour.

3 Coincidentally, this is very close to E. Birley's centurial length of 22yds (Birley 1939, 219-36).

CHAPTER 10

1 Wilmott (1997). It is reasonably clear that the first fort was turf and timber, followed by a stone fort with two breaks in its construction, all within Hadrian's reign.

BIBLIOGRAPHY

ANCIENT SOURCES

Bede *Ecclesiastical History of the English People*
Cato *de agriculturi*
Hero *Mechanica*
Josephus *Jewish Wars*
Pseudo-Hyginus *de munitionibus castrorum*
Scriptores Historiae Augustae
Codex Theodosianus
Vegetius *Epitoma rei militaris*
Marcus Vitruvius Pollio *The Ten Books on Architecture*

ABBREVIATIONS

AA[1-5]	*Archaeologia Aeliana*, 1st-5th Series
AJ	*The Archaeological Journal*
CIL	*Corpus Inscriptionum Latinarum*
CW[1-3]	*Transactions of the Cumberland and Westmorland Antiquarian and Archaeological Society* First to Third Series
BAR	*British Archeological Reports*, British and International Series
PSAN[1-5]	*Proceedings of the Society of Antiquaries of Newcastle upon Tyne*, 1st-5th series
PSAS	*Proceedings of the Society of Antiquaries of Scotland*
RIB	*Roman Inscriptions of Britain* Vol. 1

MODERN SOURCES

General works
Bidwell, P. (ed.) *Hadrian's Wall 1989-1999* (Carlisle, 1999).

Breeze, D.J. and Dobson, B. *Hadrian's Wall* 4th edition (2000).

Collingwood, B.J. *The Roman Wall* (1851).

Breeze, D.J. (ed.) *Handbook to the Roman Wall* 14th edition (Newcastle upon Tyne, 2006).

CHAPTER BIBLIOGRAPHIES

Excavation reports are not normally included unless there is specific reference to them in the text; almost all excavation reports relating to the Wall are to be found in *Archaeologia Aeliana* and the *Transactions of the Cumberland and Westmorland Antiquarian and Archaeological Society*. Publications referred to in one chapter are not repeated in later chapters to which they might also be relevant.

1. INTRODUCTION

Balaam, N. 'Pollen analysis' *AA*[5] xi (1983) 76-7.

Birley, R. *The early wooden forts* Vindolanda Research Reports, New Series, Volume III (Bardon Mill, 1994).

Dark, K. and Dark, P. *The Landscape of Roman Britain* (Stroud, 1997).

Dumayne, L. 'The effect of the Roman Occupation on the Environment of Hadrian's Wall' *Britannia* xxv (1994) 217-24.

Elton, H. *Frontiers of the Roman Empire* (1996).

Groenman-van Waateringe *et al.* (eds) *Roman Frontier Studies* Oxbow Monograph 91 (Oxford, 1997).

Hanson, W.S., Daniels, C.M., Dore, J.N., and Gillam, J.P. 'The Agricolan supply base at Red House, Corbridge' *AA*[5] vii (1979) 1-98.

Hill, P.R. 'The development of the Stanegate' in P.R. Hill (ed.) *Polybius to Vegetius* (2002) 87-102.

Hodgson, N. 'Relationships between Roman frontiers and artificial frontiers' in Groenman-van Waatering *et al.* (1997) 61-6.

Huntley, J.P. 'Paleobotanical investigations' *Britannia* xix (1988) 160-62.

Huntley, J.P. 'Environmental evidence from Hadrian's Wall' in Paul Bidwell (ed.) *Hadrian's Wall 1989-1999* (Carlisle, 1999) 48-64.

Huntley, J.P. and Stallibrass, S. 'Plant and vertebrate remains from archaeological sites in northern England' *Research Report No. 4, Architectural and Archaeological Society of Durham and Northumberland* (Durham, 1995).

Johnson, G.A.L. *The Geology of Hadrian's Wall* Geologists' Association Guide No. 59 (1997).

Jones, G.D.B. and Woolliscroft, D.J. *Hadrian's Wall from the air* (Stroud, 2001).

Lamb, H.H. 'Climate from 1000 BC to 1000 AD' in M. Jones and G. Dimbleby (eds.) *The Environment of Man: the Iron Age to the Anglo-Saxon Period* BAR 87 (1981).

Matei, A.V. 'Limes Porolissensis – a new defensive line (ditches, wall, and towers) discovered in front of the Roman military site of Porolissum, in Dacia' in Groenman-van Waateringe (1997) 93-100.

Maxfield, V.A. 'Hadrian's Wall in its Imperial Setting' *AA*⁵ xviii (1990) 1-27.

Pitts, L.F. and St Joseph, J.K. *Inchtuthil: the Roman legionary fortress excavations 1952-65* Britannia Monograph Series No. 6 (1985).

Poulter, J. 'The date of the Stanegate, and a hypothesis about the manner and timing of the construction of Roman Roads in Britain' *AA*⁵ xxvi (1998) 49-56.

Rackham, O. *The History of the Countryside* (1986, paperback edition 2000).

Seaward, M.R.D. *The Vindolanda Environment* (Haltwhistle, 1976).

Seaward, M. 'The environmental material' in van Driel-Murray *et al. The early wooden forts Vindolanda Research Report*, New Series, Volume III (Bardon Mill, 1993) 91-119.

Symonds, M. 'The construction order of the Milecastles on Hadrian's Wall' *AA*⁵ (2005) 68-81.

Walthew, C.V. 'Possible Standard Units of Measurement in Roman Military Planning' *Britannia* xii (1981) 15-35.

Watson, G.R. *The Roman Soldier* (1969).

Whittaker, C.R. *Frontiers of the Roman Empire: a social and economic study* (Baltimore and London, 1994).

Woolliscroft, D.J. *The Roman Frontier on the Gask Ridge Perth and Kinross BAR* British Series 335 (Oxford, 2002).

2. THE PLAN, AND THE START OF THE WORK

Allason-Jones, L. 'Small finds from turrets on Hadrian's Wall' in J.C.Coulson (ed.) *Military Equipment and the Identity of Roman Soldiers BAR*, International Series 394 (1988) 197-233.

Bennett, J. 'The setting, development, and function of the Hadrianic frontier in Britain' Unpublished PhD thesis, University of Newcastle upon Tyne (1990).

Bennett, J. 'The Roman Frontier from Wallsend to Rudchester Burn Reviewed' *AA*⁵ xxvi (1998) 17-37.

Bidwell, P. 'The Original Eastern Terminus of Hadrian's Wall' *AA*⁵ xxxii (2003) 17-25.

Bidwell, P.T. and Holbrook, N. *Hadrian's Wall Bridges* (1989).

Birley, E. *Research on Hadrian's Wall* (Kendal, 1961).

Breeze, D.J. and Hill, P.R. 'Hadrian's Wall began here' *AA*⁵ xxix (2001) 1-2.

Charlesworth, D. 'The Turrets on Hadrian's Wall' in Apted, M.R., Gilyard-Beer, R. and Saunders A.D. *Ancient Monuments and their Interpretation* (1977) 13-26.

Collingwood, R.G. 'Hadrian's Wall. A system of numerical references' *PSAN*⁴ iv (1931) 179-87.

Dilke, O.A.W. *The Roman Land Surveyors* (Newton Abbot, 1971).

Dobson, B. 'The Function of Hadrian's Wall' *AA*⁵ xiv (1986) 1-30.

Hargreaves, G.H. 'Roman surveying on continuous linear constructions' Unpublished PhD thesis, University of London, 1996.

Hill, P.R. 'The stone wall turrets of Hadrian's Wall' *AA*⁵ xxv (1997) 27-49.

Hill, P.R. 'Hadrian's Wall from MC0 to MC9' *AA*⁵ xxix (2001) 3-18.

Hill, P.R. and Dobson, B. 'The design of Hadrian's Wall and its implications' *AA*⁵ xx (1992) 27-52.

Hunneysett, R. 'The Milecastles of Hadrian's Wall: an alternative identification' *AA*⁵ viii (1980) 95-107.

Mann, J.C. 'The function of Hadrian's Wall' *AA*⁵ xviii (1990) 51-4.

Robertson, A.S. (revised Lawrence Keppie) *The Antonine Wall* (Glasgow 1990).

Sherk, R.K. 'Roman geographical exploration and military maps' *ANRW* II (Berlin, 1974) 534-62.

Simpson, G. 'The moving milecastle: or how Turret 0b came to be called Milecastle 1' *AA*⁵ iii (1975) 105-15.

Simpson, F.G. and McIntyre, J. 'Pike Hill' *CW* ² xxxiii (1933) 271-75.

Taylor, D.J.A. *The forts on Hadrian's Wall BAR* British Series 305 (Oxford, 2000).

Woolliscroft, D.J. 'Signalling and the design of Hadrian's Wall' *AA*⁵ xvii (1989) 5-19.

3. QUARRYING AND WORKING STONE

Behn, F. *Steinindustrie des Altertums* (Mainz, 1926).

Blake, J. *The small finds* Vindolanda Research Reports, New Series, Volume IV, fascicule III The Tools (Greenhead, 1999).

Blagg, T.F.C. 'Tools and Techniques of the Roman Stonemason in Britain' *Britannia* vii (1976) 152-72.

Dworakowska, A. *Quarries in Roman Provinces* (Warsaw, 1983).

Greenwell, A. and Elsden, J.V. *Practical Stone Quarrying* (1913).

Haselberger, L. 'The Construction Plans for the Temple of Apollo at Didyma' *Scientific American* volume 253 (December 1985) 114-22.

Haselberger, L. 'Ein Giebeliss der Forehalle des Pantheon die Werkrisse vor dem Augustusmausoleum' *Mitteilungen des Deutschen Archaeologischen Instituts*, Roemische Abteilung 101 (Mainz, 1994) 280-308.

Haselberger, L. 'Deciphering a Roman Blueprint' *Scientific American* volume 272 (June 1995) 56-61.

Hill, P.R. 'Stonework and the archaeologist: including a stonemason's view of Hadrian's Wall' *AA*⁵ ix (1981) 1-21.

Hill, P.R. and David, J.C.E. *Practical Stone Masonry* (1995).

Manning, W.H. *Catalogue of Romano-British Ironwork in the Museum of Antiquities, Newcastle upon Tyne* (Newcastle, 1976).

Manning, W.H. 'The Iron Objects' in Frere, Sheppard *Verulamium Excavations Volume III* Oxford Committee for Archaeology, Monograph No. 1 (1984) 83-106.

Parsons, D. (ed.) *Stone: Quarrying and Building in England AD 43-1525* (Chichester, 1990).

Peacock, D.P.S. and Maxfield, V.A. *Mons Claudianus: survey and excavation Volume 1 Topography and Quarries* Institut Français d'Archéologie Orientale (Le Caire, 1997).

Röder, J. 'Zur teknik der römischen Granitindustrie' in Jorns W. *Der Felsberg im Odenwald* (Kassel and Basel, 1959) 17-38.

Susini, G. *The Roman Stonecutter* (Oxford 1973).

Ward-Perkins, J.B. 'Quarrying in Antiquity; Technology, Tradition and Social Change' *Proceedings of the British Academy* lvii (1971).

Warland, E.G. *Modern Practical Masonry* (1929) (and shortened edition 1953).

Williams, J.H. 'Stone building materials in Roman Britain' unpublished M.A. thesis University of Manchester 1968.

4. LIME, SAND, AND MORTAR

Cowper, A.D. *Lime and Lime Mortars* (first published 1927 for BRE, reprinted Donhead St Mary, 1998).

Dix, B. 'The manufacture of lime and its uses in the western Roman empire' *Oxford Journal of archaeology* 1(3) (1982) 331-43.

Jackson, D.A. 'A Roman Lime Kiln at Weekley, Northants' *Britannia* iv (1973) 128-40.

Lynch, G. 'Lime Mortars – time for reappraisal?' *Architects and Surveyors Institute Journal* (March 1998) 26-7.

Lynch, G. 'Lime Mortars for Brickwork: Traditional Practice and Modern Misconceptions – Part Two' *Journal of Architectural Conservation* 4(2) (July 1998) 7-19.

Rayment, D.L. and Pettifer, K. 'Examination of durable mortar from Hadrian's Wall' *Materials Science and Technology* 3 (December 1987) 997-1004.

Vicat, L.J. *Mortars and Cements* (facsimile reprint Donhead St Mary, 1997).

5. SCAFFOLDING

Barker, P. *et al.* *The Baths Basilica Wroxeter* (1997).

DeLaine, J. The baths of Caracalla *Journal of Roman Archaeology*, Supplementary Series No. 25 (Portsmouth, Rhode Island, 1997).

Kenyon, K.M. *Excavations at the Jewry Wall Site* (Leicester, 1948).

Salzman, L.F. *Building in England down to 1540* (Oxford, 1952).

Thatcher, A.G.H. *Scaffolding* (1907).

6. HOISTING

Drachman, A.G. *The Mechanical Technology of Greek and Roman antiquity* (1963).

Hodges, H. *Technology in the Ancient World* (New York, 1992).

Landels, J.G. *Engineering in the Ancient World* (Berkley and Los Angeles, 1978).

O'Connor, C. *Roman Bridges* (Cambridge, 1993).

Singer, C., Holmyard, E.J., Hall, A.R. and Williams, T. *A history of technology* (Oxford, 1956).

7. TRANSPORT

Adams, J.N. 'The generic use of mula and the status and employment of female mules in the Roman world' *Rheinisches Museum für Philologie* Neue Folge 136. Band, Heft 1 (1993).

Armitage, P. and Chapman, H. 'Roman Mules' *London Archaeologist* 3/13 (1979) 339-59.

Audoin-Rouzeau, F. La taille du boeuf domestique en Europe de l'antiquité aux temps modernes *Fiches d'ostéologie animale pour l'archéologie*, Série B: Mammifères, No. 2 (Juan-les-Pins, 1991).

Burford, A. 'Heavy transport in classical antiquity' *The Economic History Review*, 2nd Series, xiii (1960) 1-18.

Constable, C. 'The mule as a military animal, Part II' *Exercitus* 2, 6 (1983) 73-4.

Crofts, J. *Packhorse, Waggon and Post* (1967).

Dent, A. *Donkey: the story of the Ass from East to West* (1972).

van Driel-Murray, C. 'The Roman Army Tent' *Exercitus* volume 2/8 (1990) 137-44.

Essin, E.M. *Shavetails and Bellsharps* (Lincoln USA, 2000).

Ewart, J.C. 'Animal remains' in J. Curle *A Roman Frontier Post and it's People* (Glasgow, 1911) 362-77.

Meek, Professor A. and Gray, R.A.H. 'Animal remains' *AA*[3] vii (1911) 143-267.

Hulme, S. *Native Ponies of the British Isles* (Hindhead, 1980).

Hyland, A. *Equus: the horse in the Roman world* (1990).

Kendal, R. 'Transport Logistics Associated with the Building of Hadrian's Wall' *Britannia* xxvii (1996), 129-52.

Lee, John 'The last of the carrier Galloways' *PSAN*[4] x (1946) 332-34.

Lepper, F. and Frere, S. *Trajan's Column* (Gloucester, 1988).

Lewis, M.J.T. 'The Origins of the Wheelbarrow' *Technology and Culture* 35(3) (July 1994) 453-75.

Mayes, Bill 'The Reconstruction of a Leather Tent' *Exercitus* 2(10) (1994) 183-86.

Sherlock, D. 'Roll out the barrow' *Building* 22/29 (1978) 22-3.

Spruytte, J. *Early Harness systems* (1983).

Thompson, F.M.L. (ed.) *Horses in European Economic History* (1983).

Veterinary Department *Animal Management* (1908).

8. BUILDING OPERATIONS

Heyman, J. *Structural Theory of Masonry* Paperback edition (Cambridge, 1997).

Ling, R. 'The mechanics of the building trade' in F. Grew and B. Hobley (eds) *Roman urban topography in Britain and the western empire* CBA Research Report No 9 (1985).

Smith, H.P. B.Sc. (Eng.), M.I.Struct.E. *Constructional Archwork* (1946).

Warburton, J. *Vallum Romanum* (1753).

9. ORGANISATIONAL ASPECTS OF THE WORK

Birley, E. 'Building records from Hadrian's Wall' *AA*[4] xvi (1939) 219-36.

Birley, E.B. 'The fate of the Ninth Legion' in Butler, R.M. (ed.) *Soldier and civilian in Roman Yorkshire* (Leicester, 1971) 71-80.

Birley, E. 'Hyginus and the First Cohort' *Britannia* xii (1981) 287.

Birley, A.R. *Hadrian: the restless emperor* (1997).

Bowman, A.K. *Life and Letters on the Roman Frontier* (1994).

Bowman, A.K. and Thomas, J.D. *Tabulae Vindolandensis II* (1994).

Breeze, D. 'The organization of the legion: the first cohort and the equites legionis' *JRS* lix (1969) 50-5.

Fink, R.O. *Roman Military Records on Papyrus* (Cleveland, Ohio, 1971).

Frere, S.S. 'Hyginus and the First Cohort' *Britannia* xi (1980) 51-60.

Hooley, J. and Breeze, D. 'The Building of Hadrian's Wall: a reconsideration' *AA*[4] xlvi (1968) 97-114.

Richmond, I. A. and Birley, E. 'Centurial stones from the Vallum west of Denton Burn' *AA*[4] xiv (1937) 227-42.

Stevens, C.E. The Building of Hadrian's Wall *CW Extra Series* XX (Kendal, 1966).

War Office *Manual of Field Engineering* HMSO 1911.

War Office *Field Service Pocket Book* HMSO 1914.

War Office *Military Engineering Vol. V* (War Office, 1935).

War Office *Military Engineering Vol. II* (War Office, 1936).

10. DISLOCATION

Casey, J. 'The coinage of Alexandria and the Chronology of Hadrian' in Huvelin H., Christol M., and Gautier G. *Mélange de Numismatique* (Wetteren (Belgium), 1987) 65-72.

Charlesworth, D. 'Housesteads west ditch and its relationship to Hadrian's Wall' *AA*[4] xlix (1971) 95-9.

Crow, J.G. 'A review of current research on the Turrets and Curtain of Hadrian's Wall' *Britannia* xxii (1991) 51-63.

Heywood, B. 'The Vallum – its problems restated' in M.G. Jarrett and B. Dobson (eds) *Britain and Rome* (Kendal, 1965) 86-94.

Hill, P.R. 'Hadrian's Wall: some aspects of its execution' *AA*[5] xix (1991) 33-9.

Jarrett, M.G. 'An unnecessary war' *Britannia* vii (1976) 145-51.

Shaw, R.C. 'Excavations at Willowford' *CW*[2] xxvi (1926) 429-506.

Wilmott, T. *Birdoswald: Excavations of a Roman fort on Hadrian's Wall and its successor settlements: 1987-92* English Heritage Archaeological Report 14 (1997).

INDEX